MY STORY
Jesus

F. Arthur Coombes

F. Arthur Coombes

MY STORY (JESUS)

ISBN-10: 1-897373-98-8
ISBN-13: 978-1-897373-98-9

Printed by Word Alive Press

 WORD ALIVE PRESS
Just Write!

131 Cordite Road, Winnipeg, Manitoba, R3W 1S1
www.wordalivepress.ca

Contents

Preface

The story you hold in your hand was written nearly 2000 years ago by four men inspired by God to record the central facts about Jesus' life while he was clothed in human flesh here on planet earth. They each recorded the message of Jesus in their own distinctive way, sometimes borrowing from each other accounts they deemed necessary as the Holy Spirit guided. Most events are described with different incidental details in each gospel. In recent times, men have arranged these four books in parallel columns, trying to harmonize them into a time-line. The order of many of the events here is not important, however, as one soon realizes when examining the four texts. Many of Jesus' teachings would have been repeated over the time of his ministry so the contexts would vary.

One soon realizes some interesting things about these records. God gave the authors considerable freedom as they set out to describe Jesus' life. They have a genuine human touch. At the same time, the unity of the message is unmistakable. There is no question about who Jesus is or what he taught. Matthew and Mark harmonize well. Luke has many similar records but in a different order. John records a lot of discourses of Jesus not included in the other gospels. This story contains the texts of all the gospels. The account of Zechariah entering the Holy Place comes partly from Alfred Edersheim's description of the temple worship in The Life and Times of Jesus.[1] The actual words of Jesus follow the original text very closely, so they reflect what he

---

[1] Alfred Edersheim, *The Life and Times of Jesus the Messiah Vol 1* (New York, Longmans, Green, and Co., 1905), 133ff.

intended. Everything is written from a high view of Biblical inerrancy.

My Story

Prologue
(John 1:1–5, 9–14, 16–18)

In the beginning I was the Word. I was with God and I was God. In the beginning, at creation, I was with God. I was the Word who spoke everything into existence. Nothing was made without me. I was the source of life which gives light to everyone. The light shines in the darkness and nothing can put it out. I am the true light that brings truth to every man; I was about to come into the world.

Even though the world was made through me, men didn't recognize me when I came. Even my own people, the Jews, did not accept me. But to all who did accept me, believing in my name (Jesus), I gave the right to become children of God. They are actually born all over again. This is not a human plan; this is a direct act of God.

So I took on human flesh and lived here among all of you. You saw my glory, glory that can only come from my Father because I am his exact likeness. I was filled with unlimited grace and truth just like my Father. Being clothed in human flesh did not make me any less God than I was when I commanded the universe into existence.

From my endless supply you all received favor on top of favor. Moses gave you the Law, but I brought my loving favor and my integrity of person. None of you have ever seen the living God, but I came directly from my Father's embrace. My presence gave you an intimate living picture of his essential character.

John the Baptist
(John 1:6–8; Luke 1:5–7)

My Father sent a man and named him John. He was sent to testify about my coming into the world. John was not the light; he was only a witness to my coming so that men would be prepared to believe in me.

My Father chose Zechariah and Elizabeth to be John's parents. He chose them because they were both upright, faithfully obeying His commandments. He knew Elizabeth's heartache because she had no children. They were both very old.

I will let Zechariah tell you his story . . .

* * *

Zechariah's Story
(Luke 1:8–25; 57–80)

One day when my division of the priesthood was serving, I was in the temple at dawn as usual. Each day one of us was chosen by lot to enter the Holy Place to burn incense before God. I was startled to find that the lot fell on me. Everyone in the temple stood praying in absolute silence when the chosen priest slipped through the curtains with the incense. Trembling, I entered upon this most holy task. As I crossed the holy place to the altar, I poured out the incense on the burning coals prepared for it. Suddenly I was aware of a light to my right. Turning, I saw a brilliant angel. I was terrified. But he said, "Do not be afraid, Zechariah. God has heard your prayers and shared your tears. Your wife, Elizabeth, will bear a son! You are to name him John. Great joy and gladness will sweep over both of you, for the Lord will hold him in high honor. Unlike any other man, he will be filled with the Holy Spirit from before his birth. He will bring repentance to many in Israel so that they will turn to the Lord. He will fulfill what Malachi predicted: 'I am sending you one with the Spirit and power of Elijah. His preaching will turn the hearts of the fathers to their children and the disobedient to accept wisdom.'"[2]

I listened in astonishment. As my mind envisioned my dear, grey-haired wife and considered my own impotence, I blurted out, "How can this happen? We are very old."

The angel's tone changed. "I am Gabriel, who stands in the very presence of God. I was sent to tell you this good news. Since you do not believe, you will be unable to speak until all that I have told you comes about."

Meanwhile, those standing outside were concerned that I was so long in the Holy Place. When I came out, I could not speak so I made signs with my hands. Then they realized I had seen a vision.

When my division was done, I went home to my wife. Things happened just as Gabriel said. For five months Elizabeth hid herself. Unable to contain her joy, she exulted, "The Lord saw my tears, shared my sorrow and confounded those who called me barren."

The day finally came when Elizabeth was to deliver her son. All the family and neighbors rejoiced with her when they heard of God's great mercy upon her. On the eighth day when it was time to circumcise the boy, they all gathered, expecting to call him Zechariah after me. Elizabeth spoke up, "No, no, he shall be called John."

They were all taken back. "No one in your entire family has that name!"

They all turned to me to find my thoughts on the matter. I called for a writing tablet and wrote, "His name is John!" They could hardly believe their eyes. Immediately I was able to speak again; the neighbors were awestruck.

The story spread throughout the Judean hill country. "What will this child become?" many wondered. Already the Lord's hand was with him.

I was so filled with the Holy Spirit that I prophesied as I stood among them:

---

[2] Malachi 4:5–6

"Praise to the Lord God of Israel,
For he has visited us.
He has redeemed his people.
As the prophets foretold,
From David's line
A powerful Redeemer has come.
We shall be saved from our enemies;
Those who hate us will fail.
He shall fulfill the promises to our fathers,
The holy covenant sworn to Abraham.
In holiness and righteousness we shall serve
Without fear all the days of our lives."
Cradling my son, I continued,

"And you, my child,
Shall be the promised prophet chosen by God
To prepare the way for our Redeemer,
To proclaim the dawn of salvation to his people
Through sins forgiven by God's tender mercy.
The light of the new day shall release those sitting in darkness;
In the shadow of death, our feet shall be led in the way of peace."

Our child grew strong in spirit, led into the wilderness by the Lord in preparation for his unveiling to the people of Israel.

* * *

Announcement to Mary
(Luke 1:26–38)

When Elizabeth was six months along in her pregnancy, my Father sent the angel Gabriel to a virgin named Mary living in Nazareth in Galilee. She was engaged to a man named Joseph, a descendant of David. Gabriel appeared to her, saying, "Blessings on you, most favored woman! The Lord is with you!" Trembling, she wondered what this greeting could possibly mean. "Calm your fears, Mary. God's favor rests upon you. You are going to become pregnant. The son you bear, you must call him Jesus. He will be very great, for he will be the Son of the Most High. God will give him the throne of his forefather, David. He will rule over the descendants of Jacob forever; his reign will never end."

Mary was even more puzzled. "How can this happen? I don't even have a husband."

Gabriel continued, "The Holy Spirit will come upon you and the power of the Most High will overshadow you, so that your child will be called Holy, the Son of God. And how about this—your relative, Elizabeth, is six months pregnant with a son in her old age, yet! Everyone called her barren but nothing stops God's plan, for with God nothing is impossible.

Mary responded, "I am the Lord's slave. May he do as you have said." Then Gabriel left.

Mary Visits Elizabeth
(Luke 1:39–56)

Mary wasted no time going to see Elizabeth. She hurried off to Zechariah's home in the hill country of Judah. Coming to the house, she greeted Elizabeth. When Elizabeth heard Mary's greeting, her baby leaped in her womb. The Holy Spirit came upon Elizabeth so that she shouted out,

"Most blessed are you of all women
And blessed is your offspring.
Why should I be so privileged
That the mother of my Lord should visit me?
When I heard your greeting
My baby leaped for joy within me!
She is blessed who believed
That the message from the Lord would be fulfilled by him."

Then Mary spoke,

5

"In my soul I lift up the Lord and
In my spirit joy overflows at every thought of God, my Savior,
For he has chosen me,
A maiden of humble birth,
To bestow great things upon me—
So great, all future generations
Will call me blessed.
Holy is his name,
the Almighty who has done this.
Since the earth began
His favor has rested
On those who stand in awe of him.
His arm reached out in power,
His face against the proud,
Their imaginations in disarray.
The powerful, he has toppled;
The powerless are enthroned.
The hungry have been filled,
The rich emptied.
Israel he has helped;
His abundant mercy revealed
His words to our fathers, confirmed
To faithful Abraham and his children forever."

Mary stayed with Elizabeth for about three months before returning home to Nazareth.

My Birth
(Matthew 1:18–25; Luke 2:1–7)

My mother, Mary, was engaged to a man named Joseph. But before they married, Mary became pregnant through the Holy Spirit so Joseph had to decide what to do. He was a just man, so he decided to break the engagement quietly because he didn't want to publicly disgrace her. Even as Joseph was considering this, my Father sent an angel to him. The angel appeared in a dream and said to him, "Joseph, son of David, don't be afraid to take Mary and marry her, for the child she is carrying has been conceived by the Holy Spirit. She is going to have a son and you must name him Jesus, for he will save his people from their sins."

All this took place exactly as God had revealed to the prophet Isaiah: "Behold a virgin shall conceive and bear a son. His name shall be called Emmanuel (which means, 'God is with us'.)"[3]

When Joseph woke up, he did just what the angel told him. He took Mary to be his wife but she remained a virgin until I was born.

Just before the time of my birth, an order went out from Caesar Augustus requiring everyone to be registered in a census of the entire Roman Empire. This was the first census when Quirinius was governor of Syria. Everyone went to the city of their origin to be registered.

As Joseph was a descendant of King David, he had to go to Bethlehem, the city of David. So he took Mary and they arrived shortly before she was to deliver. Bethlehem was so crowded there was no room in the inn, so when Mary delivered me, she had to lay me in a manger. She wrapped me in strips of cloth as was the custom.

The Shepherds
(Luke 2:8–20)

Near Bethlehem, some shepherds were guarding their sheep during the night. Suddenly a brilliant light shone all around them and an angel stood before them. They were terrified until the angel spoke: "Do not be afraid. I have come to announce wonderful news, news that will bring great joy to the hearts of people all over the world. This very day a Savior has been born in the city of David. He is Christ the Lord. You can confirm my message by going into town. You will find a baby wrapped up and lying in a manger."

---

[3] Isaiah 7:14

Suddenly the entire sky was brilliantly lit up by a multitude of angels, all praising God. Their voices reverberated all around the shepherds as they called out, "Glory to God in the highest and on the earth peace to all who please Him."

The shepherds were awestruck as they watched the angels ascending into the night sky. Once more they were alone, still overcome by the glory they had seen and heard. When they found their voices, they all expressed the same thoughts: "We have to go to Bethlehem to see this child the Lord has told us about."

Their legs could scarcely keep up with their excitement! As they rushed into Bethlehem, they soon found Mary and Joseph in the stable and me lying in the manger. Their words tumbled over one another as they tried to express to Mary and Joseph all they had seen and heard. Anyone who met those shepherds wondered what it all could mean. Shepherds weren't known to carry on this way!

Their story confirmed to Mary the amazing miracle of my birth. She thought long and deeply about these things as she stored them up in her heart.

As for the shepherds, they praised God all the way back to the flock. They would never be the same as they glorified God wherever they were. Even the sheep must have known something had happened.

My Circumcision and Consecration
(Luke 2:21–24)

At the end of eight days I was circumcised. I was given my name, Jesus, at that time, the name given by the angel to Mary before I was conceived.

When Mary had completed her time of purification, they came to the temple in Jerusalem to consecrate me to the Lord (at 40 days).[4] That was in accord with the law of the Lord: "Every male that opens the womb shall be called holy to the Lord." So

---

[4] Exodus 13

they offered the required sacrifice: "a pair of turtledoves, or two young pigeons."[5]

Simeon
(Luke 2:25–35)

A righteous and devout man named Simeon lived in Jerusalem in those days. He eagerly looked forward to the coming of the advocate for Israel. The Holy Spirit was with him and told him that he would live to see the Messiah, the Christ of God.

The Spirit inspired him to come into the temple at just the right time to meet Mary and Joseph as they brought me in to dedicate me as the Law required. Simeon took me up in his arms and praised God, saying,

"Lord, I'm ready to come home.
You have fulfilled your promise;
I've seen the Savior with my own eyes.
He's here for all to see,
And he is one of us.
For the nations, his light overcomes the darkness;
He brings glory to Israel."

Joseph and Mary stood in amazement at Simeon's words.

Simeon went on to bless them. Then turning to my mother, he said: "In Israel, many will fall while others will rise because of him. He will be an unwelcome sign to those who speak against him, for the very thoughts of many will be revealed. A sword will also pierce your own soul."

Anna
(Luke 2:36–39)

In the same hour, a prophet, Anna, came up to them. She was the daughter of Phanuel, of the tribe of Asher. She lived

---

[5] Leviticus 12:1–8

with her husband for only seven years from her virginity. Now she was very old, living as a widow for eighty-four years. She never left the temple; night and day she never ceased to worship, fast and pray. She gave thanks to God, speaking about me to everyone around whom she knew was also looking for the deliverance of Jerusalem.

When Joseph and Mary had done all that the Law required, they left Jerusalem.

The Wise Men
(Matthew 2:1–12)

I was born in Bethlehem in the days of Herod the king. While we were still there, wise men came from the east to Jerusalem. They inquired, "Where is the child who has been born king of the Jews? We saw his star in the east so we have come to worship him."

When Herod heard this news, he was extremely upset. When Herod was upset no one else in Jerusalem could sleep either! Herod assembled the chief priests and scribes, asking them, "Where is the Christ to be born?"

They answered, "In Bethlehem, right here in Judea. This is how the prophet Micah predicted it: 'and you, Bethlehem, in the tribe of Judah, are certainly not least among the rulers of Judah, for a ruler shall come from you who will govern all my people Israel.'"[6]

Herod hatched a plan to get rid of this threat. He arranged a secret meeting with the wise men. Pretending devotion, he asked when the star had appeared. Gathering that information, he sent them on their way with these words: "Go and search diligently for the child. When you have found him, come and tell me. Then I will also come and worship him."

Leaving Herod, the wise men went on their way. Amazingly, the star they saw in the east guided them all the way to Bethlehem, even to the house where we were staying. Their

---

[6] Micah 5:2

hearts leaped up when they saw the star, so much so that they rejoiced all the way to Bethlehem. When they came into the house, they saw me with my mother, Mary. They immediately fell on the floor and worshipped me. They brought beautiful gifts, real treasures of gold, frankincense and myrrh. When they were getting ready to return, they were warned in a dream not to go back to Herod. So they went home by a different route.

To Egypt
(Matthew 2:13–18)

When the wise men had gone, an angel appeared in a dream to Joseph with an urgent message: "Get up. Take the child and his mother and escape to Egypt. Stay there until I tell you. Herod is going to come looking for the child to destroy him."

Joseph wasted no time. He got up in the middle of the night, took me and my mother and headed for Egypt. We stayed in Egypt until the death of Herod. This fulfilled what my Father said through the prophet: "Out of Egypt I have called my son."[7]

When Herod realized he had been tricked by the wise men, he flew into a furious rage. Remembering what the wise men told him about when they saw the star, he determined to slaughter all the baby boys two years old and under in and around Bethlehem. This fulfilled the message spoken by Jeremiah, the prophet:

"A cry was heard in Ramah,
Weeping and loud laments,
Rachel weeping for her children.
She could not be comforted because they were gone."[8]

---

[7] Hosea 11:1
[8] Jeremiah 31:15

From Egypt
(Matthew 2:19–23; Luke 2:40)

After Herod died, an angel instructed Joseph in a dream, saying, "Pack up. Take the child and his mother and return to Israel. Those who plotted to kill him are dead."

So Joseph took me and my mother and left Egypt. When we arrived in Israel, Joseph found out that Herod's son, Archelaus, was now ruling in Judea. Joseph realized the danger. My Father also warned him in a dream, so he returned to Nazareth, in Galilee, his home town. Even this was predicted by the prophets: "He shall be called a Nazarene."

I continued to grow, becoming strong and full of wisdom. My Heavenly Father's favor rested upon me.

My Youth
(Luke 2:41–52)

My parents went to Jerusalem every year for the feast of the Passover. When I was twelve, we went as usual. When the feast was over, they began the journey home, as always, in the company of all our friends and relatives. Unknown to them, I stayed behind in Jerusalem. Assuming I was among the large throng, they travelled most of the day before they realized I was nowhere to be found. No one had seen me. There was nothing left to do but to return all the way back to Jerusalem.

After three days, they finally found me sitting in the temple among the teachers. I was fascinated listening to them and being able to ask them questions in return. I wasn't aware of how unusual it was for a boy of my age to understand them and be able to ask intelligent questions in response. Anyone within hearing was amazed at my understanding.

It was so fulfilling, I lost all sense of time until my distraught parents arrived on the scene. I saw the utter frustration on my mother's face coupled with the relief of at last finding me. My being in the presence of all these learned teachers must have softened what she otherwise might have said! So she unloaded the best way she could: "Son, why have you treated us this way?

Your father and I are at our wits' end. We have been looking for you for three days!"

My reply must have sounded completely off the wall to them. They were not ready for what came next. I answered in a way that seemed perfectly obvious to me: "How come you looked for me? Don't you know I must be in my Father's house?" Having said that, I knew that I had to be obedient to them. So I got up and went with them back to Nazareth. My mother thought long and hard about these things, for she now knew in her heart that I had already reached beyond my human parents.

John the Baptist's Ministry
(Matthew 3:1–12; Mark 1:2–8; Luke 3:1–18)

In the fifteenth year of the reign of Tiberius Caesar, John the Baptist began his ministry in the wilderness around the Jordan River.

His message: "Repent, for the kingdom of God is near." All those who repented and confessed their sins, John baptized in the river. It was a baptism of repentance.

John's work was foretold by the prophets:

"Listen, I am sending my messenger ahead of you."[9]
"The voice of one shouting in the wilderness:
Straighten the paths,
Fix the road,
Fill up the gullies,
Level the hills,
Make the way smooth.
Everyone shall see the salvation of God."[10]

John wore a robe of camel's hair with a leather belt around his waist. He ate locusts and wild honey. People went out to hear him from Jerusalem, all over Judea and the area around the

---

[9] Malachi 3:1
[10] Isaiah 40:3–5

Jordan. They confessed their sins and John baptized them in the Jordan River.

Eventually John saw many of the Pharisees and Sadducees coming for baptism. He had a stern word for them: "You nest of snakes! Who warned you to escape the coming judgment? Baptism won't mean anything unless your life reveals true repentance. Don't think that being children of Abraham will guarantee your future. I tell you, God can raise up better children of Abraham from these stones. Already, the axe is chopping at the base of the trees that do not bear good fruit. Soon they will be thrown into the fire."

Hearing these things, the crowds asked, "What should we do?"

John replied, "If you have two coats, give one to someone who has none. Do the same with food." Even the tax collectors came, asking the same questions. John told them, "Don't collect more than you are supposed to." To soldiers, he said, "Don't take advantage of people, using your power to violently rob them or to invent false accusations for your own gain. Instead be content with your wages."

The powerful work of the Spirit through John brought new hope to the people. Some began to think that maybe he was the Messiah. When John became aware of these thoughts, he quickly made it clear he was not the Messiah: "I baptize you with water, but after me one is coming who is so much greater than I am that I am not even worthy to untie his sandals. His baptism will not be just with water but with the Holy Spirit and with fire. He is ready to bring in the harvest. He will separate the wheat from the chaff; the wheat he will keep for himself, but the chaff will burn with unquenchable fire."

My Baptism
(Matthew 3:13–17; Mark 1:9–11; Luke 3:21–23)

Before setting out on my ministry, I left Nazareth and went down to John to be baptized. When John saw me coming, he objected. "I should be baptized by you. Why are you are coming to me to be baptized?"

I responded, "Do not object, John. I understand how you feel. In doing this, we are fulfilling all that's right." John nodded and we both stepped down into the river. As I stood up again in the river, I raised my head and looked toward my Father and prayed, knowing there was now no turning back.

At that moment, I saw a beautiful dove, wings outstretched, feet spread for a landing on my head. It was the Holy Spirit, and the thrill of his presence filled my entire being. Then I recognized the familiar voice of my Father, "This is my beloved Son who brings me endless pleasure!" I was about thirty years old at the time.

My Temptation by Satan
(Matthew 4:1–11; Mark 1:12–13; Luke 4:1–13)

As I left John, the Holy Spirit led me into the wilderness. I was there for forty days without food. The animals of the dessert were my company as I fasted and prayed. At the end of that time I became conscious of my hunger.

Satan saw his opportunity. "Since you are supposed to be the Son of God, all you have to do is command these stones to become bread and, presto, you have food."

He knew how tempting that thought had become. It sounded so simple and so logical. But I knew very well the diabolical purpose behind it. I instantly replied, "It is written, 'Man shall not live by bread alone, but by every word that comes from the mouth of God.'"[11]

Then Satan transported me to the very highest point of the temple. As we looked down, he said, "Since you are the Son of God, why don't you jump down? Is it not written, 'He will charge his angels to guard you; they will hold you up so you won't strike your foot against a stone'?"[12]

I threw back at him, "It is also written, 'You shall not tempt the Lord your God.'"[13]

---

[11] Deuteronomy 8:3

[12] Psalm 91:11–12

[13] Deuteronomy 6:16

Satan made one more try. He took me to the top of a very high mountain. In one moment, he caused all the kingdoms of the world and their splendor to pass before my eyes. He exclaimed, "All this has been given to me and I can give it to anyone I please. All you have to do is bow down here at my feet and worship me for a minute and it will all be yours."

I scarcely waited for him to finish his speech before I sent him packing. "Get out of here, Satan! It is written, 'You shall worship the Lord your God and him only shall you serve.'"[14]

Satan left, but I knew it was only the beginning of his schemes. As I sat down on a rock, exhausted, angels gathered around to minister to me.

John's Testimony
(John 1:15, 19–34)

John was baptizing at Bethany on the east side of the Jordan when the Jews sent a delegation of priests and Levites from Jerusalem to him on a fact-finding mission.

"Who are you?" they demanded.

He knew where they were going, so he immediately confessed, "I am not the Christ."

"Who are you, then? Elijah?"

"No, I am not."

"Maybe you're the prophet?"

John raised his voice, "No!" He was tired of questions.

The delegation was getting frustrated. "Be patient with us. We can't go back to the Pharisees without an answer," they pleaded. "How would you describe yourself?"

"Tell them this: I am a voice calling out in the wilderness to all who will listen, just as Isaiah said, 'Make a straight highway for the Lord.'"[15]

They pressed in, "Under what authority are you baptizing, then? You tell us you are not the Christ, Elijah or the prophet."

---

[14] Deuteronomy 6:13
[15] Isaiah 40:3

John responded, "I only baptize in water. I am preparing the way for one you do not even know yet. He is so much greater than I am; I don't even have the right to remove his shoes."

The very next day, John spotted me coming toward him. Pointing my way, he called out to the crowds, "All of you, look! Here is the one I have been telling you about. Look at him! He is the Lamb of God who cleanses the world of all its sin. He is the one I said is far greater than I am. Although I have been sent before him, he existed long before I was ever born. When I began baptizing with water, I did not even know him. Yet his coming is the entire purpose of my baptizing with water, that I might reveal him to Israel."

John went on to testify, "I saw the Holy Spirit come down in the form of a dove and it landed on him. That's how I know he is the one, because he who sent me to baptize told me, 'The Holy Spirit will come down and remain on the one who will baptize with the Holy Spirit.'

"I can assure you he is the Son of God, for I saw the sign exactly as it was promised."

First Disciples
(John 1:35–51)

A day later, John was standing with two of his disciples. As I walked by, John pointed me out, "Look, there is the Lamb of God!" Then the two disciples turned to follow me.

When I saw them, I asked, "What do you want?"

"Where are you staying?" they answered.

"Come and see," I said, so they spent the rest of the day with me.

One of these men was Andrew, the brother of Simon Peter. Immediately Andrew found his brother, Simon. He told him, "We have found the Messiah." He then brought Simon to meet me. As I studied him, I said, "So you are Simon, the son of John? You shall be called Peter." (Which means 'rock').

The next day I chose to go to Galilee. I found Philip, who was from the same town as Andrew and Peter, Bethsaida. I said to him, "Come, follow me."

Then Philip looked for Nathanael. He rushed up to him. "We have found the one Moses and the prophets told us about: Jesus of Nazareth, son of Joseph."

"From Nazareth?" asked Nathanael in disbelief. "Can anything good come from Nazareth?"

But Philip wasn't discouraged. "Come and see for yourself."

As I saw Nathanael coming toward me with Philip, I remarked, "Here comes an honest Israelite, indeed—a man with a true heart."

Nathanael heard me. "How do you know me?"

"I saw you under the fig tree before Philip called you."

Nathanael was amazed. "Teacher, you really are the Son of God, the King of Israel!"

"You believe just because I said I saw you under the fig tree? You shall see greater things than these. I tell you, you will see heaven opened and the angels of God going up and down upon the Son of Man."

The Wedding at Cana
(John 2:1–12)

On the third day after John proclaimed me as Messiah, my mother was going to be a guest at a wedding. It was in the town of Cana, in Galilee. I was also invited along with my disciples. Before the celebration was over, the wine ran out. My mother said to me, "They have no wine."

"Is this our concern, mother?" I replied. "It isn't my time yet."

She just carried on like I knew she would. She turned to the servants, "Do whatever he tells you."

Six large stone water jars were standing close by. They each held as much as thirty gallons of water (113 liters). I told the servants to fill them up with water and they did—right to the brim. Then I said, "Draw some out with your jugs and take it to the host."

When the host took a sip, he smiled and his eyes lit up. He excitedly called the bridegroom, "Everyone serves their best wine first, afterward bringing out the poorer stuff, but you have kept the best wine until now!" The servants stood there amazed, knowing that the best wine was only water a minute before.

This was the first public miracle I did. My disciples had the first glimpse of my glory and they believed in me. After this we all went down to Capernaum, on the shore of the Sea of Galilee. My mother and my brothers came with us and we stayed there for several days.

Cleansing the Temple
(John 2:13–25)

As the Passover approached, I went up to Jerusalem. As usual, the Court of the Gentiles was full of people selling oxen, sheep and pigeons for the sacrifices. The money-changers were there, charging exorbitant rates. I had seen it all before, but this time I could no longer stand it. My spirit rose within me, so I marched out and found some strong cords. I wove them into a whip and returned to the temple. The merchants recoiled in horror as I descended on them, eyes full of fire, whip flying, the cattle stampeding and the sheep running. As they escaped down passageways and out doors, I turned to the greedy money-changers. I deliberately picked up their little moneybags, pouring the contents all over the floors. Neat piles of coins soon scattered across aisles as I tipped tables. Not one of them dared touch me; they were too busy anyhow, scrambling to retrieve the only things they cared about. Nearby were the cages of pigeons. Over the pandemonium, I shouted at their owners, "Get these things out of here. You are not going to turn my Father's house into a market."

My disciples stood open-mouthed; they had never seen me like this! Then they remembered the Scripture, "Passion for your house consumes me."[16] The common people watched; some were amused while others cheered. Few had any love for those greedy traders.

---

[16] Psalm 69:9

The Jewish leaders marched up, boiling inside. What to do? The moral ground was cut from under them. They dared not arrest me, so they turned to a familiar tactic: "What miracle can you perform to prove you have authority to do this?"

The ultimate miracle that would prove my authority was yet to come, so I said, "Destroy this temple, and in three days I will raise it up."

They were baffled. "It has taken forty-six years to build this temple. Now you are claiming you can rebuild it in three days?" They had no idea I spoke of my body.

Later, when I had risen from the dead, my disciples remembered I had said this. For them, it confirmed the Scripture and the word I had spoken.

While I was in Jerusalem at the Passover, many did believe in my name because of the miracles I did. Knowing how fickle people were, though, I didn't put any faith in them. Their support could disappear as fast as it came.

Nicodemus Comes by Night
(John 3:1–21)

Nicodemus was a Pharisee, a man of high status, for he was a member of the Sanhedrin, the ruling body of the Jews. He came to me one night, since at night was the only time I wasn't surrounded with people.

"Teacher," he stated, "we know that God has sent you. No one can do the miracles you do without God."

I replied, "For certain, no one will ever see the kingdom of God unless he is reborn from above."

Nicodemus was taken back. "How can that be? You mean a man must re-enter his mother's womb and be born when he is old?"

"One must be born of water and the Spirit to ever enter the kingdom of God. Flesh can only give birth to flesh, and one born of the Spirit is spirit. Don't be surprised that I said you must be reborn from above. You can hear the wind blow but you can't tell where it's coming from or where it is going. That is exactly how it is with anyone born of the Spirit."

"How can this be?" asked Nicodemus.

I responded, "You are a teacher in Israel. Shouldn't you be able to understand this? What I am telling you is absolute truth. We only speak what we know is true, and we only tell about what we have actually seen. In spite of this, you do not accept our witness. If I tell you of facts here on earth and you cannot believe them, how can you hope to believe heavenly truth when I tell you? No one alive here on earth has ever gone up to heaven, except the One who has come down from heaven, the Son of Man.

"Just as Moses lifted up the bronze serpent in the wilderness,[17] the Son of Man must be lifted up, so that anyone who trusts in him will have life everlasting. God loved the world so much he sacrificed his only Son so that anyone who trusts in the Son will never die, but will be ushered into life everlasting.

"God did not send his Son down to earth to bring judgment on all who are on it. No! The very opposite, in fact; he sent him down to free everyone from being condemned. Whoever trusts in the Son is set free, but sadly, many refuse to trust and so have sealed their own condemnation. Nothing more can be done for them because they have turned their back on God's offer of his only Son. The reason men will be judged is because the light has shone in the world. But many hate the light because they love their evil deeds. In fact, many who do evil run from the light because it exposes how awful their deeds really are. In contrast, those who practice truth are drawn to the light because it shows that what they do is in accord with God's will."

John: "I Must Decrease"

(John 3:22–36)

After the Passover, my disciples and I travelled in Judea, where we stayed for a while, baptizing.

---

[17] Numbers 21:9–21

At the same time, John was baptizing at Aenon, near Salim, because of the abundance of water there. People continued to come to be baptized. John had not yet been imprisoned. An argument started between John's disciples and a Jew concerning purification.

John's disciples reported to John, "Teacher, the man who was with you on the far side of the Jordan, the one you testified about, also baptizes and all kinds of people are going to him."

John replied, "No one can receive anything unless God gives it to him. You have heard me say that I am not the Christ; I have been sent before him. You know how it is in a wedding—the bride goes with the bridegroom because she belongs with him. The best man, as the bridegroom's friend, hears his voice and rejoices. In the same way I rejoice. He must increase, but I must decrease. The one who comes from heaven is above all of us. We who are of the earth speak from our earthly experience. The one from above shares his heavenly experience. People do not believe his witness because their human thinking cannot grasp the truth from heaven that he shares. Those who do recognize that his testimony is true certify that God is true. He who has been sent by God speaks the very words of God because he has been given the Spirit without limit. The Father loves the Son; he has put everything in his hands. Whoever believes in the Son already has life everlasting. Whoever disobeys the Son will never even glimpse life; he will bear the weight of God's wrath on him."

John Imprisoned
(Matthew 4:12; Luke 3:19–20; John 4:1–3)

John had reproved Herod the governor for taking Herodias, his brother's wife. John also pointed out many other evil things Herod had done. As if this wasn't enough, Herod added to his sins by putting John in prison.

The news came to me that John had been arrested. Added to this, the fact that I had been baptizing more people than John came to the Pharisees' attention. (Actually I did not do the baptizing; my disciples did.) I was moved by the Spirit to leave Judea and return to Galilee.

The Samaritan Woman
(John 4:4–42)

On my way to Galilee, I chose to go through Samaria, where I came to the city of Sychar. Jacob's well was near the field that Jacob had given to his son, Joseph. It was about noon when I sat down beside the well. We were all tired from the heat and the long walk, but my disciples agreed to go into Sychar to buy food while I rested by the well. While I sat, a Samaritan woman came with her water jar. I was thirsty, so I asked her for a drink. She was amazed because Jews normally had nothing to do with Samaritans.

"You are a Jew! You're asking me, a Samaritan woman, to give you a drink?"

I said to her, "If you only knew the gift God wants to give you and who I am who asked you for a drink, you would have been the one asking me and I would have given you living water."

She looked me over, "Sir, this well is very deep and you have nothing to draw with. Where do you plan to get this living water? Are you greater than our ancestor, Jacob, who gave us the well and drank from it himself, along with his sons and cattle?"

I explained further, "Everyone who drinks from this well will soon thirst again. Anyone who drinks the water I am speaking of will never thirst again. More than that, he will have a source of this living water within himself leading to eternal life."

I really had her attention now! "Sir, that's the kind of water I want. I would never have to come here to draw again. Imagine— I would never get thirsty."

It was time to change the subject, "Go and get your husband and come back."

She said hesitantly, "I have no husband."

So I began to reveal my insights: "You answered honestly. It's true you don't have a husband. But you have had five husbands. The man you live with now is not your husband, so your answer is accurate."

As I spoke, she put her hand over her mouth and her eyes widened. She fidgeted, fearfully trying to squirm out of my gaze. When she found her tongue, she said, "Sir, I see that you are a prophet." She went on, desperate to change the topic, "Our fathers worshipped on this mountain. You Jews claim that Jerusalem is the place to worship."

I assured her, "Woman, believe me, the time is coming when you won't need to worship on this mountain or in Jerusalem. Your worship is lacking in knowledge. The Jews do worship what is true, for salvation comes from them. Worship of God is not limited by time or place, for God is spirit. All those who want to truly worship him must do so in spirit and in truth."

The woman responded, "I know that the Messiah is coming, the Christ. When he comes he will reveal everything."

I now made a direct statement to her that I very rarely said to anyone. Touching the middle fingers of my right hand to my chest, I said, "I am he, the very person who is speaking to you right now."

Just then my disciples arrived. They stared in disbelief when they saw I was talking with a woman. The unspoken questions were in their eyes, "What do you want from her?" "Why are you talking to her?" But none of them said anything.

For her part, the woman just left her water jar by the well and hurried into the city. She exclaimed to everyone she met, "Come and see a man who told me everything I've ever done. Can he be anything less than the Christ?" They all started coming out of the city toward me.

Meanwhile, my disciples brought out the food, saying to me, "Teacher, you need to eat."

I responded, "I have food you don't know about."

They turned to one another as they said, "Who has brought him food?"

I explained, "My food is to do the will of him who sent me; I am to finish his work. You would normally say, 'Isn't it four months yet to harvest time?'" As I gestured toward the city behind them, I went on, "I tell you, look over there and see how the fields are white, ready for harvest. Those who reap and gather fruit for eternal life receive wages. The sower and reaper then rejoice together. In this case, the saying holds true, 'One sows and another reaps.' I sent you to reap where others did all the labor of planting. You reaped the result of their work."

By this time the Samaritans began arriving. Many believed in me because the woman shared her simple testimony, "He told me everything I have ever done."

The Samaritans asked me to stay with them, so we stayed for two days. As they listened, many more of them believed in me. They said to the woman, "At first we believed your testimony, but now we have heard him ourselves. We now know for sure that he is indeed the Savior of the world."

Arrival in Galilee
(Luke 4:14–15; John 4:43–45)

After two days, we carried on to Galilee. As we went along, I remarked that a prophet has no honor in his own country. But when we got to Galilee, I was welcomed because they had seen all that I did in Jerusalem at the feast, for many of them had been there.

The news of my return spread throughout the entire area. Being propelled by the power of the Spirit, I preached in many of their synagogues. They accepted me wherever I went.

The Official's Son Healed
(John 4:46–54)

I came again to Cana, where I had made the water into wine. At Capernaum there was an official whose son was very sick. He got the news that I had returned to Galilee, so he immediately came as fast as possible to Cana. He begged me to come and heal his son, for the boy was near death.

I said to him, "You people will not believe unless I do signs and wonders."

At his wit's end and with tears in his eyes, he pleaded, "Sir, please come down before my child dies!"

My heart went out to him. I immediately said, "Go, your son will live." He didn't even hesitate; he believed me and started home. The next day as he was still travelling, his servants met him. Excitedly, they reported, "Your son is well; he is alive!"

"When did he get better?"

"Yesterday, at the seventh hour, the fever left him all at once."

Thinking back, the father said, "That's exactly when Jesus said to me, 'Your son will live.'" The official and his entire household believed. This was the second sign I did upon returning to Galilee from Judea.

Rejected at Nazareth
(Luke 4:16–30)

Eventually I arrived in Nazareth, my home town. As my custom was, I went to the synagogue on the Sabbath day. I stood up to read, so they handed me the scroll of the prophet Isaiah. As I unrolled it I came upon this text: "The Spirit of the Lord empowers me, for he has anointed me to preach good news to the poor, to announce release to the captives, to recover sight to the blind, to liberate the oppressed, to proclaim the favorable year of the Lord."[18]

I closed the scroll, returned it to the attendant and sat down. The eyes of everyone in the synagogue were fixed on me. I opened my mouth and began, "Today, the Scripture I just read has been fulfilled and you have heard it."

They were amazed at the gracious words they heard me speak. They spoke well of me, saying to one another, "Isn't this Joseph's son?"

---

[18] Isaiah 61:1–2

I continued, "No doubt you will quote me this proverb, 'Doctor, heal yourself,' and say, 'We have heard all the wonderful things you did in Capernaum, now do them here in your hometown.'

"It is a true saying, no prophet is accepted in his own country. Look at Elijah during the drought that lasted three-and-one-half years, bringing on a great famine in Israel. There were many widows in Israel, but where was Elijah sent? He was sent to a widow in Zarephath, in the land of Sidon.[19] The Lord never sent him to a single widow in Israel. Elisha was another example. There were many lepers in Israel in his day, but the only leper he cleansed was Naaman, the Syrian."[20]

When they heard this, the gracious words were forgotten. The entire synagogue erupted in fury and they drove me out of the city. They then took me to the brow of the hill the city was built on, intending to throw me down the cliff. But I passed through the middle of them and went on my way.

At Capernaum
(Matthew 4:13–16)

After leaving Nazareth, I went down to Capernaum, by the sea, and lived there. Isaiah foresaw this in the prophecy my Father gave him: "The darkness shall not go on forever in the land of Zebulun and Naphtali, Galilee of the Gentiles. The people who sat in darkness have seen a great light, and for those who sat in the land where death casts its shadow, light has dawned."[21]

The Great Catch of Fish
(Matthew 4:17–22; Mark 1:14–20; Luke 5:1–11)

From this time on, I began to preach, "Repent, for the kingdom of God is near." As I stood on the shore of Galilee,

---

[19] 1 Kings 17:8–24
[20] 2 Kings 5:1–14
[21] Isaiah 9:1–2

people pressed upon me to hear the word of God. I noticed two fishermen washing their nets, their boats pulled up on shore. I got into one of the boats, which turned out to be Simon's. The other boat belonged to Andrew, his brother. I asked Simon to pull out a little from the beach. So I sat in his boat and taught the people from there.

When I had finished speaking, I turned and said to Simon, also called Peter, "Put out into deeper water and drop your nets to catch some fish."

Simon looked at me wearily and, with a tired voice, replied, "Master, we fished all night and didn't even get a single fish. But because you have asked, I will let down my net." We moved out from shore and the men lowered the nets overboard. Simon suddenly came to life. His nets were so full of fish there was no way they could haul them into the boat. As they tried, the nets began to break, so he waved to the other boat to come and help. The fish filled both boats so full they began to sink.

Simon Peter had been a fisherman far too long to not recognize the finger of God, so he fell at my feet, begging, "Please leave me, Lord, for I am a sinful man." All the fishermen stood in astonishment. That included James and John, sons of Zebedee, who were partners with Simon.

I said to Simon, "Don't be afraid. From now on you are going to catch men."

When the boats were brought to land, I said to them, "Follow me." Immediately they left their nets and followed me. James and John pulled in just along the shore. I called them too, and they left everything with their father and the servants and followed me. We went into Capernaum.

Demon-Possessed Man Healed
(Mark 1:21–28; Luke 4:31–37)

On the next Sabbath, I entered the synagogue in Capernaum and began to teach. My teaching amazed the people because I spoke with authority. The scribes who usually taught did not do this; they always quoted famous teachers. I taught for a while, but then I was interrupted by a man possessed by an unclean spirit. He shouted out, "Why are you bothering us, Jesus of Nazareth? Have you come to destroy us? I know who you are, the Holy One of God."

I reproved him, saying, "Be quiet; come out of him at once!" The unclean spirit threw the man on the floor and, crying out with a loud voice, came out of him. The man was not harmed.

This really stirred the people up. They said to one another, "What kind of teaching is this? Who is this who commands evil spirits with authority and power? They even obey him." People spread this story all over Galilee so that I became well known.

Peter's Mother-in-law Healed
(Matthew 8:14–15; Mark 1:29–31; Luke 4:38–40)

When I left the synagogue, I went to the home of Simon and Andrew. James and John were also with me. Simon's mother-in-law was sick with a fever. When I saw her, I stood over her and rebuked the fever. Taking her hand, I lifted her up and the fever left her. With joy she got up and served us.

Other Healings
(Matthew 8:16–17; Mark 1:32–34; Luke 4:40–41)

That same day when the Sabbath was ending at sunset, the people came to me with any that were sick or possessed with demons. The whole city was gathered at the door. I cast out the demons with a word, and I laid hands on any that were sick and they were all healed. The demons often cried out, "You are the Son of God!" but I did not permit them to speak because they knew who I was.

All of this was a fulfillment of what Isaiah said: "He took away our illnesses and carried off our diseases."[22]

---

[22] Isaiah 53:4

Leaving Capernaum for a Time
(Matthew 4:23–24; Mark 1:35–39; Luke 4:42–44)

Early the next morning—long before sunrise—I went out of the city to a lonely place to pray. The people were looking for me, so Simon, along with the others, followed where I went. They said, "Everyone is searching for you."

I replied, "I need to go on to the other towns to preach the good news of the coming of the kingdom of God, because that is why I came."

So we went all over Galilee. I preached and taught in the synagogues about the gospel of the kingdom. I healed every disease of those who came to me, and I cast out demons.

Healing a Leper
(Matthew 8:2–4; Mark 1:40–45; Luke 5:12–16)

In one of the towns, a man full of leprosy saw me. He rushed over, fell on his face in front of me and pleaded, "Lord, if you so desire, you can make me clean."

My heart was moved with pity at the sight of him, so I reached out and touched him, saying at the same time, "I do so desire; be clean." Immediately, the leprosy was gone and he was restored to normal. I reminded him to show himself to a priest and to bring the offering prescribed by Moses for his cleansing, as this proved to the people that he was clean.[23] I added, "Whatever you do, don't tell anyone about your healing."

Unfortunately, he went out and told everyone he had been healed. The result was I could not even enter a town because of the crowds, so I stayed out in the open country and people came to me from all over. When I could, I withdrew into the wilderness to commune with my Father.

---

[23] Leviticus 14

The Paralytic Lowered through the Roof
(Matthew 9:1–8; Mark 2:1–12; Luke 5:17–26)

Later I returned to Capernaum in a boat. News soon spread that I was back home. So many gathered that they could not come in the house; many stood outside near the door. Pharisees and teachers of the Law came from every town in Galilee and even as far away as Judea and Jerusalem. As I was teaching them, I sensed a power to heal from my Father. A group of four men came, carrying a paralyzed man on his bed. They wanted to lay him before me, but they soon realized there was no normal way to get him there. So they took him up on the roof and proceeded to make an opening. They lowered him down in front of me, bed and all. When I saw what faith they had, I said to the paralyzed man, "My son, your sins are forgiven."

Some of the scribes and Pharisees sitting there began questioning in their hearts, "Who does this man think he is? This is blasphemy; only God can forgive sins."

I read their thoughts, so I immediately addressed them. "Why do you think evil in your hearts? Which is it easier to say, 'Your sins are forgiven,' or 'Rise, take up your bed and walk'? To prove to you that the Son of Man has authority to forgive sins here on earth, I will show you my authority to heal." So I turned and, looking down at the paralyzed man, I said, "Get up, pick up your bed and walk." Immediately he stood up and picked up his bed. Right there he began praising God as he joyfully pranced out of the room.

Fear came over the crowd when they saw this. Filled with awe and amazement, they praised God. "We have never seen anything like this, that God would give a man such authority."

Matthew Called
(Matthew 9:9–13; Mark 2:13–17; Luke 5:27–32)

I left the house and went out by the seashore, where the crowd that followed gathered around me as I taught. When I was done, I headed back into town, where I came upon Matthew (also called Levi), the son of Alphaeus. He was sitting at the tax office as he was a tax collector. I looked him in the eye and, reaching out my hand toward him, I said, "Come, follow me." Right away, he got up and followed me. This called for a celebration, so he invited me and my disciples to a great feast at his house. All his friends were there—fellow tax collectors and many others of uncertain reputation.

The Pharisees, who would never soil their reputation with such riff-raff, avoided me and complained to my disciples, "Why do you and your teacher eat with these tax collectors and sinners?"

I overheard them, so before my disciples could speak, I addressed them directly. "Those who are healthy don't need a doctor, only those who are sick. Go and learn what this means: 'I desire mercy, not sacrifice.'[24] I did not come to call the righteous to repentance but those who are sinners."

John's Disciples Come
(Matthew 9:14–17; Mark 2:18–22: Luke 5:33–39)

John's disciples noticed that my disciples did not fast like they and the Pharisees did. So they came to me, asking, "Why do we and the Pharisees fast but your disciples do not fast?"

I replied, "Can you make wedding guests fast when the bridegroom is there? The day will come when the bridegroom is taken away from them and then they will fast."

To help them understand what my coming into the world meant, I used an illustration. "No one puts a patch of new, unshrunken cloth on an old garment, because if you do, when you wash it the patch will shrink and tear the garment worse than before. In the same way, no one puts new wine into old wineskins, because if you do, the old skins will burst and the wine will be lost. New wine must be put into new wineskins. Men who have savored the old wine don't like the new. They won't change over."

---

[24] Hosea 6

Miracle on the Sabbath in Jerusalem

(John 5:1–18)

It was a time of feasting for the Jews, so my disciples and I went down to Jerusalem. There was a pool called Bethesda near the Sheep Gate. It had five porches full of disabled people: lame, blind and paralyzed. They were there because of a tradition that an angel of the Lord came occasionally and touched the water. The first person in afterward would be healed.

I noticed a man lying there that I knew had been there a long time, so I asked him, "Do you want to be healed?"

He replied, "Sir, I have no one to put me into the pool when the water is touched, so someone always gets in before me."

So I said to him, "Take up your bed and walk."

He was instantly healed, so he rose up, picked up his bed and walked away. He didn't get far before some Jews intercepted him. "It is the Sabbath. It is against the Law to carry your bed on the Sabbath."

The man explained, "The man who healed me told me to take up my bed and walk, so I did."

"Who told you to pick up your bed and walk?" He didn't know who I was because there was a large crowd at the pool and I had slipped away unnoticed.

Later I came upon the man in the temple, so I said to him, "You have been healed. Sin no more, so that nothing worse happens to you."

The man went away and told the Jews I had healed him. The upshot of this was that the Jews persecuted me all the more. My answer to them was, "My Father is working still, and I am working." By this time, the Jews were looking for an opportunity to kill me, not only because I healed on the Sabbath, but also because I called God my Father, thus making myself equal with God.

The Controversy

(John 5:19–47)

Now that they understood I called God my Father, I went on to explain further. "I tell you the absolute truth. I, the Son, can do nothing on my own; I do only what I see my Father doing. Whatever he does, I do the same. My Father loves me, so much so that he reveals to me all that he, himself is doing. He will reveal to me even greater works than you have seen so that you will be amazed. For even as my Father gives life to whoever he wishes—even raising the dead to life—so I, the Son, will also give life to whomever I desire. My Father does not even pass judgment on any one; he has given all judgment to me, the Son. He has done this that all may honor the Son even as they honor the Father. Whoever does not honor the Son dishonors the Father who sent him.

"I tell you this eternal truth: whoever hears my word and believes God who sent me possesses life everlasting. That person will never come under judgment but has already passed from death to life. In fact, the time is coming and is already here when the dead will hear the voice of the Son of God. Those who hear will live. As my Father has life inherent in himself, so also he has given me, the Son, life inherent in myself. My Father has given me authority to pronounce judgment because I am the Son of Man.

"Don't be amazed at this. The time is coming when everyone in the graves will hear my voice. The good will come out to experience life; evildoers will come out to face judgment.

"Again I tell you, I can do nothing on my own authority. I judge according to what I hear. My judgment is truly just because I don't go about seeking to do my own will. My judgment rests entirely on the will of my Father who sent me.

"When I testify concerning who I am, you do not think it is true. But there is someone else who testifies concerning me. I know that his testimony is true. You even sent messengers to John the Baptist and his testimony was the truth, not that the testimony I receive comes from man. I say these things that you might be saved. John was a lamp that kept on burning and shining. You willingly enjoyed his light for a time. But I have a witness far greater than John's. The works that my Father has commissioned me to carry out, these are the evidence that proves my Father has sent me. On top of that, my Father who sent me has born witness to me himself. You have never heard his voice, neither have you ever seen his form. His word has no place in you; that is proven by the fact you do not believe me, the Son whom he has sent.

"You continually search the Scriptures because you feel sure you will find eternal life through them. These Scriptures testify about me, the one who brings life, yet you do not receive me when I come bringing the very life you are looking for. I do not come hoping to win a popularity contest; I don't accept honor from men. I know the love of God does not live in you, because I come in the Father's name and you do not recognize me. When others come, glorifying their own names, you receive them readily enough. How can you hope to recognize the true One when you puff yourselves up, seeking honor from one another? The only authentic honor comes from the one true God, and you don't seek that.

"Don't get the idea I am planning to bring accusations against you to my Father. You already stand condemned before Moses, the one you set your hope in. If you really believed Moses, you would believe me because he wrote about me. If you don't believe Moses, what hope is there that you will believe me?"

Eating Grain on the Sabbath
(Matthew 12:1–8; Mark 2:23–28; Luke 6:1–5)

One Sabbath, as I was going through the grain fields with my disciples, they became hungry, so they began pulling off heads of grain. They rubbed them in their hands to eat the kernels. When the Pharisees saw them, they were indignant. "Don't you see what your disciples are doing? To do that is unlawful on the Sabbath!"

I replied, "Have you never read what David did when he was hungry? He entered the house of God and ate the bread of the Presence, which is unlawful for anyone to eat except the priests.[25] Or haven't you read in the Law how the priests working in the temple on the Sabbath break the Law and yet are guiltless? I assure you, someone greater than the temple is here. The Sabbath was made for man, not man for the Sabbath. The Son of Man is Lord even of the Sabbath."

Withered Hand Healed
(Matthew 12:9–21; Mark 3:1–12; Luke 6:6–11)

One Sabbath when I entered a synagogue, there was a man with a withered right hand. As I taught, the scribes and Pharisees were watching closely to see if I would heal him regardless of the fact that it was the Sabbath. It deeply troubled me that the religious leaders should be so utterly uncaring. I knew their thoughts, so I wasn't surprised when one of them spoke up, "Is it lawful to heal on the Sabbath?" I knew it wasn't an honest question; they had long since decided that issue. They wanted to trap me.

As my eyes scanned their hard faces, I turned to the poor man. "Come up and stand here." Hope lit up his face as he bounced up beside me. I addressed the gathering, "It's my turn to ask you: is it legal on the Sabbath to do good or to do harm, to save or destroy life?" Of course, they were silent. An honest answer would have revealed their cold, calloused hearts to everyone present.

I went on, "Who is there here that, if his sheep fell into a pit on the Sabbath, wouldn't reach down and lift it out?" Again, not a sound in the entire room; everyone knew the answer. After the pause, I said, "If a sheep is worth rescuing, surely a man is, for he is worth infinitely more than a sheep. The only reasonable conclusion then: It is lawful to do good on the Sabbath." By this time my eyes flashed in anger, while at the same time I felt deeply grieved that nothing moved them.

---

[25] 1 Samuel 21:1–6

Turning to the man, I said in a gentle tone, "Stretch out your hand." Even as he did, it was completely restored.

The Pharisees were furious. It was written all over their faces as they stomped out of the synagogue. They got together with the Herodians, spending the rest of the Sabbath plotting how to kill me.

Aware of their plots, my disciples and I left there and went down to the Sea of Galilee. Great crowds followed us, not only from Galilee but also from beyond Jordan, Jerusalem, Judea and even Tyre and Sidon. I had healed many, so people pressed in upon me just to be able to touch me and be healed. Unclean spirits caused people to fall down in front of me, crying out, "You are the Son of God." I strictly ordered them to be quiet. As I stood on the lake's shore, I told my disciples to get a boat ready, for the crowd was crushing in upon me.

All of this fulfilled what Isaiah had predicted: "Look upon my servant whom I have chosen, my beloved who rejoices my soul. I will put my Spirit in him without limit. He will proclaim justice to the nations. He will not argue or loudly challenge. No one will hear his voice raised in the streets. He will not even break off a bent reed nor quench a smoldering wick until he brings justice to all the earth. On his name the nations will rest their hope."[26]

Picking Out the Twelve
(Matthew 10:2–4; Mark 3:13–19; Luke 6:12–16)

To escape the crowds, I went out into the hills, where I spent the whole night communing with my Father. As the sun peaked over the horizon, I called my disciples. From among them, I chose twelve to be with me. They would become the sent ones (apostles) who would be sent out to preach and to have authority to cast out demons. Here are their names:

Simon, whom I named Peter

---

[26] Isaiah 42:1–4

Andrew, Simon's brother
James, the son of Zebedee
John, the brother of James
(I called James and John "sons of thunder.")[27]
Philip
Bartholemew, also called Nathanael
Thomas
Matthew, the tax collector
James, the son of Alphaeus
Simon, the Zealot
Thaddeus, also called Judas, son of James
Judas Iscariot, my betrayer

Sermon on the Mount
(Matthew 5:1–7:29; Luke 6:17–49; 12:22–31)

One day when I saw the crowds gathering, I went up on a mountainside with my disciples. I sat down and began to teach.

"How blest are those who know they are spiritually needy, for my Father will give them the kingdom.

"How blest are those who weep over unrighteousness, for my Father will dry their tears.

"How blest are those who quietly restrain themselves when provoked, for the earth will be their inheritance.

"How blest are those who hunger and thirst for uprightness, for they shall be filled up.

"How blest are those who extend forgiveness, for they shall be forgiven.

"How blest are those whose hearts are pure, for my Father shall delight in welcoming them into his presence.

"How blest are those who make peace, for my Father will call them his children.

"How blest are those who are ill-treated for doing what is right, for my Father will welcome them into the joys of the kingdom of God.

---

[27] John 1:45

"You will be blest when men pour insults upon you and abuse you and spread all kinds of lies about you because you belong to me. Jump for joy because the reward my Father will pour out upon you in heaven will exceed anything you could imagine in your wildest dreams. The prophets before you were treated the same way, so you will belong to their illustrious company."

(Luke 6:24–26)

"But what sorrows await you that are rich, for you already have your joys.

"What sorrows are coming to you who are full of yourselves now, for your hollowness will become evident and you will find nothing to fill the void.

"What sorrows will overtake you who laugh your way through your pleasure-filled life, for you shall weep as you grieve over your wasted years forever.

"What sorrows will come to you who live for the praise of men, for their approval is the same as the false prophets received in their time."

(Matthew 5:13–37)

"You are the salt of the earth, but if salt loses its ability to preserve and enhance taste, how can it be restored? It's useless except to be thrown out on the path to be walked on.

"You are the light of the world, a city on a hill-top that cannot be hidden. Men don't light a lamp only to put it under a bucket. Of course not—they put it on a stand so it gives light to the whole house! In the same way, let your light shine before men so they can see the good you do and give glory to your Father in heaven.

"You may think I have come to set aside the Law and what the prophets wrote, but it is just the opposite; I have come to fulfill them in the true sense. This is the absolute truth. Heaven and earth will pass away before a single dot on an 'i' or cross on a 't' will be erased from the Law until it is all fulfilled. Whoever sees no need for one of the least of these commandments and teaches others the same will be called least in the kingdom of God. Whoever obeys the Law and teaches others the same will be called great in the kingdom of God. For I tell you, unless your righteousness is greater than that of the scribes and Pharisees, you will never even enter the kingdom of God.

"You have heard the Law given to men centuries ago, 'You shall not kill.'[28] Whoever kills will be liable before the court, but I am telling you that anyone who is angry with his brother is liable before the court. Whoever insults his brother will be liable before the high court, and whoever says, 'you fool' to anyone is in danger of going to hell. So if you are about to offer your gift at the altar and you remember your brother has good reason to hold something against you, leave your gift right there and go and be reconciled to your brother first; then offer your gift.

"If someone is accusing you of something and has already set a court date, go immediately to him and make things right. The judge may agree with him and levy a heavy fine or send you to jail. You will not be free of him until you have paid every penny.

"You know that the Law also states, 'You shall not commit adultery.'[29] I tell you that everyone who only looks at a woman and then lusts over her has already committed adultery with her in his heart. If your right eye causes you to sin, cut it out and throw it away. It's better to lose one of your parts than to have your entire body thrown into hell. In the same way, if your hand leads you to sin, cut it off—throw it away!—because it is better to lose a hand than have your entire body thrown into hell. Moses also taught you, 'Whoever divorces his wife, let him give her a certificate of divorce.'[30] But I tell you, whoever divorces his wife, except on the grounds of immorality, makes her an adulteress. Whoever marries a divorced woman commits adultery.

---

[28] Exodus 20:13
[29] Exodus 20:14
[30] Deuteronomy 24:1, 3

"You know that Moses said, 'A man who makes a vow to the Lord must not ever break it.'[31] I say to you, do not swear at all, either by heaven, for it is God's throne, or by the earth, for it is God's footstool, or by Jerusalem, for it is the city of the great king. Don't even swear by your head, for you can't even make one hair white or black. Let what you say be simply 'Yes' or 'No.' Anything more than this is evil."

(Matthew 5:38–48; Luke 6:27–36)

"You have read in the Law, 'An eye for an eye and a tooth for a tooth.'[32] But I say to you, love your enemies, do good to those who hate you, bless those who curse you, pray for those who mistreat you. Don't resist those who do evil. If someone strikes you on the cheek, offer the other cheek too. If anyone takes your coat, let him take your cloak as well. If someone forces you to walk one mile with him, go with him two miles. Give to those who beg from you; do not refuse them. If they take your goods, don't ask for them back. Whatever you would want men to do to you, do the same to them.

"You have heard it said, 'Love your neighbor and hate your enemy,' but my word to you is love your enemies and pray for those who persecute you. In doing these things, you act as sons of your heavenly Father. He shines the sun on the evil and the good and sends rain on the just and the unjust. If you only love those who love you, what is special about that? Even sinners love those who love them. Why should you be rewarded for that? And if you only greet those who are friends and relatives, what are you doing more than anyone else? If you lend only to those you expect will pay you back, what is special about that? Even crooks lend to those they know will pay them back. But if you lend expecting nothing back, your reward will be great, for then you are acting like your Father in heaven, who is kind even to the ungrateful and selfish. Be merciful even as he is merciful. You must be perfect as he is perfect."

---

[31] Numbers 30:1–2

[32] Leviticus 24:20

(Matthew 6:1–34; Luke 12:22–31)

"Resist every temptation to display your spiritual activity so everyone will see how righteous you are. The hypocrites even sound a trumpet when they contribute so men will praise their supposed generosity. They already have all the reward they are going to get. When you give of your means, don't even let your left hand know what your right hand is doing. Then your giving will be secret. Your Father, who secretly watches, will reward you beyond measure.

"The hypocrites even make a display of praying. They love to pray while standing in the synagogues and on the street corners so everyone can see how holy they are. They have the only reward they are going to get. When you pray, go into your room, shut the door and pray to your Father in secret. Your Father will hear and reward you accordingly.

"When you pray, don't mindlessly repeat empty phrases over and over as in other religions. Don't do like them. Your heavenly Father is fully aware of all your needs even before you ask him, so pray like this:

Dear Father in heaven,
May your name be honored all over the earth.
May your kingdom extend into all our hearts.
May doing your will become our top priority
So that here on earth it will be like a taste of heaven.
Provide our bread for the day.
Forgive our sins against others just as we forgive those who sin against us.
May your leading in our lives steer us clear of temptations, so that we will escape doing evil.

"If you forgive others who have harmed you, your Father in heaven will forgive you for the harm you have done. However, if you don't forgive others who have harmed you, your Father cannot forgive the harm you have done.

"When the hypocrites fast, they make a great show of how they are suffering. They put on their worst religious faces, wearing haggard looks like their best friends just died. They go all day in their bed-heads and with dirt on their faces like they are so holy they can no longer manage to even pick up a comb.

"When you fast, do just the opposite. Attend to your hair and wash your face. Put on your cheerful smile and greet others just as you always do. That way, no one will ever know you are fasting, but your Father in heaven will know and he will reward you handsomely.

"Don't spend your energy trying to amass wealth here on earth, where currencies fail and stock markets crash, where crooks will find ways to relieve you of it, where you may fall for get-rich-quick schemes. When your treasure is on earth, that's where your heart will be. Rather, accumulate a treasure store in heaven, where your heavenly Father will keep it safe and where he will multiply it many times. You only get to keep what you give away.

"What are your eyes like? Are they like narrow slits, watching for every opportunity to make a buck, increase your hoard and get ahead of the Joneses? If your eyes are like that, your whole body is full of darkness. But if your eyes are open wide, looking for ways to bless others less fortunate, your body will be full of light. You cannot serve two masters. You can only serve one of them, for the other becomes a kill-joy you deeply resent. If you love money, God takes a back-seat. If you serve God, money will become your servant, only incidental in your quest to use it to his glory.

"Live like you really believe you have a loving Father in heaven. Don't be anxious about what you will have to eat or what you will have to wear. Are you going to allow your needs for tomorrow to consume all the joy the Lord provides for today? Life is so much more than food and clothing.

"Look at the birds—no planting, no gathering, no hoarding. Your heavenly Father feeds them, so why would he neglect you who are much more valuable? Does anxiety add one minute to your life? Why worry about clothing? Look at these lilies—

Solomon in all his glory never wore clothing that beautiful. God covers the hillsides with such glory, yet it will soon wither and die. Your faith is so small! Don't you see he will clothe you whom he loves?

"Don't spend the rest of your days asking these questions:

What will we eat?
What will we drink?
What will we wear?

"The nations seek all these things and your heavenly Father knows you need them. Put first things first. Seek to enter the Father's kingdom; discover his righteousness and the joy of being and doing in him. Without you worrying, he will provide all these things as well. Don't worry about tomorrow. The cares you have today are enough."

(Matthew 7:1–29; Luke 6:37–49)

"Beware of setting yourself up as a judge of others; for whatever standards you load on them will come back to haunt you. You will be judged by the same standards. Whatever you hand out, you will get the same back. If you do not condemn, you will not be condemned. If you forgive, you will be forgiven. If you give, it will be given to you: full measure, pressed down, shaken together and running over—it will be poured into your lap.

"Here is a parable: Can a blind man lead a blind man? Won't they both fall into the ditch? As a disciple, beware of imagining you know better than your teacher. When one is fully taught, he will be like his teacher.

"How readily you think you can see the speck in your brother's eye while you still have a log in your own eye. You not only think you see it, you are all ready to tell him about it and to help get rid of it! You hypocrite! Until you deal with the log in your own eye, you are in no position to straighten your brother out. When you clear up the log in your own eye, then you will see clearly enough to help your brother.

"Use discretion in who you share God's truth with. Don't desecrate the holy by giving it to dogs. Don't waste pearls of wisdom on pigs; they will only trample them in the mire and then turn on you.

"When you lack knowledge, come to the Father. Simply ask and it will be given to you; seek and you will find; knock and the door will open. Everyone who asks receives, whoever seeks finds and for whoever knocks, the door will open. Which one of you would give your son a stone when he asks for a loaf? Would you give him a snake when he asks for a fish? Even you who are evil would never do that, so why do you doubt that your loving Father in heaven will give you good gifts when you ask him?

"The Law and the Prophets are summed up in this saying: Whatever you want men to do to you, you do the same for them.

"If you want to find life, enter by the narrow gate. It's easy to drift along on the wide road to destruction. You will have lots of company, all heedlessly sauntering along on the line of least resistance. The narrow gate is hard to find and the path is rugged. You won't find many on it because most people aren't even interested.

"Along the road there are many false prophets offering all kinds of things. They look like gentle sheep, but if you peel back the fleece you will discover ravenous wolves. To uncover them, you must study the fruit of their talk. Do you get grapes from thorns or figs from thistles? Good trees bear good fruit. No matter how convincing the bad tree may look, it cannot bear good fruit. The treasure of a good person's heart will produce good. The evil of a bad heart can only produce evil. Whatever the heart is full of, that is what will come out of the mouth. Not everyone who calls me 'Lord, Lord,' will enter the kingdom of God—only those who do the will of my Father in heaven.

"On that day, many will say to me, 'Lord, Lord, didn't we prophesy and cast out demons in your name? Didn't we do many great works in your name?' I will reply to them. 'I never knew you. Get out of here, you evildoers.'

"Everyone who hears my words and does them will be like a wise man who dug down and built his house on bedrock. When the big storms came with high winds, pounding rain and floods, the house stood firm because of its rock-solid foundation.

"Everyone who hears my words but never applies them will be like a foolish man who built his house on sand. When the storms came with wind, water and floods, the house soon collapsed. It was completely destroyed."

The crowds were amazed at my teaching.

Centurion's Servant Healed
(Matthew 8:1, 5–13; Luke 7:1–10)

After finishing my teaching, I returned to Capernaum. The Jewish elders approached me as I entered the city. They explained that a centurion living in the city had a very dear slave who was paralyzed—near death, in fact. They went on, "When he heard of you, he asked us to come that you might heal his slave. He is very worthy for you to come, for he loves our nation. He even built us our synagogue."

Of course I went along with them. As we neared the house, the centurion and some of his friends met us. He said, "Lord, I am not worthy to have you enter my home. You only need to say the word and my servant will be healed. I am a man under authority myself with soldiers under me. They do my bidding; whether I tell them to come or to go or to do this or that, they do it."

The man's faith astounded me. I turned to those who were following. "This is amazing. In all Israel I have not found such remarkable faith. I tell you the truth, people will come from all over the world and eat with Abraham, Isaac and Jacob in the kingdom of God, while others who are descendants of Abraham will be thrown into outer darkness. There men will weep and gnash their teeth." Turning back to the Centurion, I said, "Go; it will be done just as you have believed." The slave was healed at that very moment.

Widow of Nain
(Luke 7:11–17)

Not too long after this, I went to a city in Galilee called Nain. As my disciples and I neared the city along with a crowd, we met a funeral procession coming out of the city. We learned the only son of a widow had died. Most of the people of the city were with her.

When I saw her look of desolation and her sobbing, I was deeply troubled. I told her, "Don't cry." Then I reached out and, touching the bier, said, "Young man, I say to you, get up." The young man immediately sat up and began talking. As I directed him to his mother, her tears of desolation suddenly turned into tears of joy.

As they embraced, everyone else stood in stunned silence, the fear of the Lord coming over them. They soon broke into rejoicing, saying, "A great prophet has come to us!" and, "God has visited his people!" News of this remarkable miracle spread all over Galilee and even Judea.

John the Baptist's Question
(Matthew 11:2–19; Luke 7:18–35)

At this time, John the Baptist was in prison. His disciples told him about all the miracles I was performing. John, in his discouragement, sent a message to me by two of his disciples. He asked, "Are you the One who is to come, or should we look for another?"

While his disciples watched, I cured many diseases, restored many people's eyesight and cast out demons. I then turned to John's disciples and said, "Go and tell John what you have seen and heard: the blind see, lame people walk, lepers are cleansed, the deaf hear and the dead come to life. The good news is preached to the poor. Blessed are those who are not offended by me."

After they left, I spoke of the importance of John: "What did you expect to see when you went out in the wilderness to John? A flimsy reed bent in every direction by every breeze? Or perhaps you expected a man clothed in expensive clothes? Those who dress like that are in king's palaces.

"What, then, did you expect? To see a prophet? Yes, I tell you, and more than a prophet. He is the one predicted in the Scriptures: 'Look, I am sending my messenger before you. He shall prepare the way for you.'[33] I say to you, no parents have ever given birth to anyone greater than John the Baptist. Yet he who is least in the kingdom of God is greater than he is. Ever since the days of John the Baptist until now, the kingdom of God has been assaulted."

When I said this, the common people and the tax collectors were justified before God because they had been obedient by having John baptize them. The scribes and Pharisees, on the other hand, had rejected God's plan for them because they refused to be baptized.

I continued, "The Law and the Prophets held sway until the time of John. If you can accept it, John is the Elijah who was to come. If you are really listening, take note of what I have said. How can I describe this generation? They are like children playing in the marketplace. They call out to one another, 'We played the flute and you didn't dance; we wailed, you didn't cry.' John came neither eating bread nor drinking wine, so you said 'He has a demon.' The Son of Man came eating and drinking and you scorned him: 'Look at him, a glutton and a drunk. He's even a friend of tax-collectors and sinners.' Yet everyone defends his own version of wisdom."

The Pharisee and the Sinful Woman
(Luke 7:36–50)

One of the Pharisees invited me to eat with him, so I went to his house and reclined at the table. I had not been there long when a woman of the city discovered I was there. Her bad reputation was well known all over town. She arrived, carrying an alabaster flask of ointment. She stood behind me at my feet, weeping. Then she bent down and wet my feet with her tears and, taking her long hair, dried them with it. She kept kissing

---

[33] Malachi 3:1

my feet as she opened the beautiful flask and lovingly applied the ointment to my feet.

Simon, the Pharisee, was not impressed. He said to himself, "If this man was a prophet, he would know what kind of sinful woman is touching him."

I addressed his unspoken criticism. "Simon, I have something to say to you."

"What is it, Teacher?" he replied.

"A certain man had two debtors. One owed him 500 pieces of silver, while the other owed him 50. Neither of them could pay, so he forgave them both. Which one of them would love him the most?"

Simon, beginning to realize where this was going, grudgingly answered, "I suppose it's the one who was forgiven the most."

"Your judgment is correct." I then turned and gestured toward the woman, "Do you see this woman? When I came into your house, you never washed my feet, yet she has washed my feet with her tears and dried them with her hair. You gave me no kiss, yet she kissed my feet the whole time I have been here. You put no oil on my head, but she has anointed my feet with ointment. I assure you, her many sins are forgiven, for her love is great. He who is forgiven little loves little."

I looked directly into her tear-stained face and said, "Your sins are forgiven."

Other guests at the table began to mutter, "Who is this who even forgives sins?"

Ignoring them, I continued, "It is your faith that has saved you; go in peace."

(Luke 8:1–3)

After this I travelled through cities and towns, preaching the good news of the kingdom. The twelve went with me as well as women who had been oppressed by evil spirits and healed of diseases. One was Mary, called Magdalene, who was freed from seven demons. There were Joanna, the wife of Chuza, Herod's steward and Susanna. Many others also provided for me and my disciples from their wealth.

(Mark 3:19–21)

When I returned to Capernaum, the crowds moved in again, so much so that we couldn't even eat. My friends, hearing of this, planned to rescue me. They said to one another, "He is beside himself."

My Work Attributed to Satan
(Matthew 12:22–45; Mark 3:22–30)

One day a demon-possessed man who was also blind and unable to speak was brought to me. When I saw his hopeless condition, I was moved to heal him. When I did, he began speaking and seeing. The people were amazed. "Can this be the predicted Son of David?" they asked one another.

When the scribes and Pharisees heard this, they could not deny the miracle so they claimed, "He has to be doing this by the power of Satan, the prince of demons, who gives him power to cast the demons out."

I knew what they were saying so I gathered them around to warn them. "How can Satan cast out Satan? Whenever a kingdom becomes divided internally, it will soon be defeated. The same applies to a city; even a household will fall apart. So if Satan is divided in his own kingdom, it will soon come to an end. If I am casting out demons by Satan's power, by what power are your sons casting them out? They will become your judges. But if I am casting out demons by the Spirit of God, then the kingdom of God has come among you. No one can rob a strong man's house unless he can tie up the strong man first. Whoever is not with me is against me. There is no neutral ground; whoever doesn't gather with me scatters.

"I tell you the truth, whatever sins people commit can be forgiven, but whoever blasphemes the work of the Holy Spirit cannot be forgiven. You can say whatever you like against the Son of Man and it can still be forgiven, but attributing the work of the Holy Spirit to Satan can never be forgiven—not in this time, nor in the age to come.

"There is no middle ground. Either make the tree good and then its fruit will be good, or make the tree bad and its fruit will be bad. A tree is known by its fruit.

"You brood of snakes! How can you claim to speak good when you are evil? What you say reveals what is in your hearts. A good man brings from his good heart good things. Just the same, an evil man spreads evil.

"Now hear this. On the day of judgment, men will have to account for every thoughtless word they speak. By your words you will be either vindicated or condemned."

Some of the scribes and Pharisees asked me, "Teacher, we want to see a sign from you."

I gave them a straight answer: "An evil and adulterous generation is always looking for a sign. There will be no sign given other than the sign of the prophet, Jonah. As Jonah was three days and nights in the whale's belly, the Son of Man will be three days and nights in the middle of the earth. The people of Ninevah will condemn this generation, for they repented when Jonah preached to them and someone far greater than Jonah is standing here now. The Queen of Sheba will condemn this generation, for she came from the far south to hear Solomon's wisdom and someone far greater than Solomon is here now.

"When an unclean spirit comes out of man, he roams the desert places looking for a place to rest but he doesn't find anything. So he says to himself, 'I will return to the house I left.' When he gets there he finds it empty, orderly and all cleaned up. So he brings seven more spirits more evil than himself and they all move in. The last state of the man will be far worse than the first situation. That's how it is going to be for this evil generation."

(Matthew 12:46–50; Mark 3:31–35; Luke 8:19–21)

While I was still speaking, my mother and my brothers arrived. They could not get to me because of the crowd.

Eventually I was told, "Your mother and your brothers are standing outside wanting to see you."

I responded, "Who are my mother and my brothers?" I scanned those sitting around me. Then, pointing to my disciples, I said, "Here are my mother and my brothers. Whoever does the will of God is my brother, sister and mother."

Parable of the Sower
(Matthew 13:1–23; Mark 4:1–20; Luke 8:4–15)

After this I went out of the house and sat by the seaside. As a large crowd gathered around me, I got into a boat and sat there teaching the people, using parables. I said to them, "A sower went out to spread seed on the land. Some of it fell on the path; it got walked on and the birds ate it. Other seed fell on rocky ground where there was very little soil. It sprouted soon enough, but when the sun got hot, it withered away, for it could not get rooted. Still other seed fell in a patch of thistles. It started to grow, but the weeds grew faster, so they soon choked out the seedlings. The result was nothing matured to produce grain. The rest of the seed fell on good soil, where it continued growing. It yielded from thirty to one hundred times what was sown. You who have ears to hear what I am saying, listen carefully."

When the crowd dispersed, I was alone with my disciples. They asked me, "Why do you speak to the people in parables?"

I explained to them, "You are privileged to know the secrets of the kingdom of God, but this is not given to those outside. To them, everything is given in parables. To those who already have, more will be given; they will have abundance. Those who don't have will lose even what little they have now. That is why I speak to them in parables—so that even in what seems to be seeing, they don't see, and in hearing they don't understand.

"They are the fulfillment of Isaiah's prophecy: 'You will hear but never understand, and you will think you see but you won't see. The heart of the people has become listless; they are indifferent to what they hear; their eyes have fallen shut, so that they won't see with their eyes or hear with their ears or understand with their heart and turn for me to heal them.'[34]

"How blest are your eyes that see and your ears that hear! Understand this: many prophets and godly men longed to see what you are seeing and to hear what you are hearing but they never saw anything compared to what you are seeing or heard anything approaching what you are hearing.

"Don't you understand the parable? How are you going to understand all the other parables? Let me tell you, then, the meaning of the parable of the sower. The seed is the word of God. The sower spreads the word. Those along the path are the ones who hear but immediately Satan snatches the word from their hearts so they will not believe and be saved. The rocky ground represents those who hear the word and immediately receive it with joy, yet it doesn't take root in their hearts. As soon as troubles or ridicule or opposition come because of their faith, they drop it. As for the thistle patch, these people hear the word, but as soon as they go their way, their busy lives take over. They are consumed with making money, accumulating things and enjoying the pleasures of life. The seed never matures. But the good soil hears the word, takes it to heart and latches onto it. These are the people who bear fruit thirty to one hundred times what was sown."

(Mark 4:21–25; Luke 8:16–18)

I continued, "No one lights a lamp and then covers it with a pail or hides it under the bed. Rather, they put it on a stand so everyone can see. Nothing is hidden that shall not become known. Be careful what you hear. To the extent you give you will receive even more. From him who has not, even what he has will be taken away."

---

[34] Isaiah 6:9–10

Kingdom of God Parables
(Mark 4:26–29)

I spoke another parable to the people. "The kingdom of God is comparable with a man planting seed in the ground. He carries on with his daily life and the crop grows without him knowing how it happens. The earth supports the plants by itself until ears form and the grain matures. But once the grain is ripe, he gathers it in because it is harvest time."

(Matthew 13:24–30)

"The kingdom of God is like a man who sowed good seed in the field. However, during the night an enemy sowed weeds in the same field. When the good seed began to grow, so did the weeds. The man's servants came to him, 'Master, didn't you sow good seed? Where did the weeds come from?' He replied, 'This is the work of an enemy.' 'Do you want us to pull up the weeds?' they asked. 'No, don't do that. You will uproot the wheat too. Let them grow together until harvest. Then we can separate the weeds and burn them while we gather the wheat into the barn.'"

(Matthew 13:31–43; Mark 4:30–34; Luke 13:18–21)

"Again, the kingdom of God can be compared to a grain of mustard seed planted in the ground. It is the smallest of seeds, yet when it is full grown it becomes a large shrub with strong branches. The birds even make nests on its limbs."

I told them another parable. "The kingdom of God is like yeast that a woman mixed into a bowl of flour until it had all risen."

I spoke to them in many parables as long as they were able to listen. In fact, I didn't say anything without a parable. This fulfilled the prophecy, "I will open my mouth using parables. I will say what has been hidden since the world began."[35]

---

[35] Psalm 78:2

Having said this, I left the crowds and went into the house. Then my disciples came to me with a request. "Explain the parable of the weeds in the field."

I responded, "The one who sows the good seed is the Son of Man. The field is the world and the children of the kingdom are the good seed. The weeds are the followers of Satan; he plants them among the children of the kingdom. The harvest is the end of the age and the reapers are the angels. Just as the weeds are gathered and burned, so it will be at the end of the age. The Son of Man will send his angels to gather those who increase sin and all who do evil. They will be thrown into the fiery furnace where men will weep and gnash their teeth. Then the righteous will shine like the sun in the kingdom of their Father. If you have ears, listen."

(Matthew 13:44)

"The kingdom of God is like a treasure in a field, hidden until a man found it. Seeing it, he quickly covered it up; then he went and sold everything he had and bought the field."

(Matthew 13:45–46)

"The kingdom of God can also be compared to a merchant seeking fine pearls. He found a very rare one of great value, so he sold all that he had and bought it."

(Matthew 13:47–53)

"In another comparison, the kingdom of God is like a net thrown into the sea that gathered many kinds of fish. The fishermen dragged the full net up onto the shore, where they sorted the catch. The good fish were put in baskets while they threw the rest out. This is how it will be at the end of the age. The angels will separate the evil from the righteous and throw them into the fiery furnace, where people will weep and gnash their teeth. Do you understand what I have been saying?"

The disciples answered, "Yes."

I concluded my teaching with, "Every scribe who has been fully trained for service in the kingdom of God is like a householder who brings out new and old treasures from his storehouse." And having finished my parables, I left.

Tempest on the Lake
(Matthew 8:18, 23–27; Mark 4:35–41; Luke 8:22–25)

One day when large crowds had gathered around me and the sun was beginning to set, I said to my disciples, "Let's get into a boat and cross over to the other side." So, leaving the crowd, we set sail. I was exhausted, so before we had gone far, I fell sound asleep on a cushion in the stern. Eventually a wild storm swept down on the lake. My disciples recognized the danger as the wind howled through the rigging and waves began crashing over the boat.

When the boat began filling up and I slept on, they hurriedly woke me up. They shouted above the roar of the storm, "Master, we are about to capsize!"

I sat up and asked them, "Why are you so afraid? Have you no faith?" Then I stood up, and looking straight into the raging storm, I simply said, "Peace, be still!" Immediately the wind stopped and the waves subsided. It was so calm you could have heard a pin drop.

The disciples sat in stunned silence. The powerful reminder of who I was overwhelmed them. They looked at me and then at one another, "We thought we knew him, but who is this? All the powers of nature bow at his command. At a word, they obey him!"

Demon-Possessed Man Healed
(Matthew 8:28–34; Mark 5:1–20; Luke 8:26–39)

We soon arrived on the other side in the country of the Gerasenes,[36] across from Galilee. When we got out of the boat, we met a man[37] with unclean spirits. He no longer lived in a

---

[36] Mark and Luke use "Gerasenes" while Matthew has "Gadarines."

[37] Matthew notes "two" men.

house but in the tombs. He was so fierce that people avoided the area. They had tried to bind him with shackles and chains but he broke the chains and smashed the shackles. He would cry out, night and day, among the tombs, bruising himself with stones. He saw me in the distance and came running. He fell at my feet, crying out with a loud voice, "Why have you come here, Jesus, Son of God on High? Have you come to torment me?"

I commanded, "Come out of him, you unclean spirit!"

The spirit begged, "Please, don't torment me."

So I asked him, "What is your name?"

He replied, "My name is Legion, for we are many. Please don't send us away into the abyss." A large herd of pigs were feeding nearby, so the demons begged me, "Send us into the pigs." I allowed them to enter the pigs, so they came out of the man. The entire herd of 2,000 pigs rushed down the steep bank into the sea, where they drowned.

The herdsmen ran in terror, telling everyone in the city and the surrounding area what had happened. People started coming to see what took place. When they arrived, they saw the man calmly sitting there, fully clothed and in his right mind. The people were filled with fear, so they begged me to leave the area. When we got into the boat to return, the healed man begged to go with us. I told him he couldn't come with us, but I said further, "Go home to your friends and family and tell them what God has done for you, how he has had mercy on you." That's exactly what he did. He waved us goodbye and told his amazing story all over Decapolis. All who heard him were astounded at his testimony.

Jairus's Daughter Healed
(Matthew 9:18–26; Mark 5:21–43; Luke 8:40–56)

We returned to Capernaum. Seeing us coming, a large crowd was already on the shore welcoming us. We had just gotten out of the boat when Jairus, a ruler of the synagogue, came to me. He fell at my feet right there on the beach. "My only daughter is dying. Can you come and lay hands on her? I know you can make her well again." I agreed to go with him, so we started through the crowd in the direction of his house.

There was a woman in the crowd who had suffered through a hemorrhage for twelve years. She had spent everything on many doctors but to no avail. When she heard about me, she said to herself, "Even if I can only touch the hem of his garment, I will be healed." The crowd was pressing me on every side, but in her desperation, she squeezed through until she was behind me. Reaching through between the moving bodies, she managed to touch my robe. Immediately her bleeding stopped; she could tell because she felt the healing touch in her body.

I knew right away that power had gone out of me, so I turned around and asked, "Who touched my robe?"

My disciples gave me strange looks. Peter exclaimed, "People are pressing against you on all sides, and you are asking, 'Who touched me?'"

Then I clarified, "Someone touched me in a special way because I felt power go out from me." As I looked around at those standing nearby, they all denied it was them. When the woman realized she had been detected, she came up to me, trembling, and fell at my feet. Frightened and embarrassed, she haltingly explained everything. Looking at her there and hearing of all her suffering, my heart went out to her. With compassion in my voice, I said, "Don't be afraid, daughter; it's your faith that has made you well. Go in peace."

While I was still speaking, someone came from Jairus's house, saying, "Don't trouble the teacher any more; your daughter is dead."

Ignoring their report, I said to Jairus, "Do not fear. Just believe and your daughter will be well."

When we arrived at his house, I would not allow anyone to accompany me except Peter, James and John. Inside it was like a zoo. There were flute players and a whole army of mourners, weeping and loudly wailing, as was the custom. I said to the crowd, "Why all the weeping and wailing? She is not dead, she only sleeps." They all laughed at me because they knew she was dead. I ordered them all outside and, after considerable complaining, they finally left. Then I went into the girl's room with my three disciples and her parents. I took her hand in mine and said to her, "Little girl, I say to you, get up." She immediately got up and started walking (for she was twelve years old). I told them to give her something to eat. Her parents were overcome with joy and amazement, but I told them not to tell anyone what happened.

Two Blind Men and a Possessed Man Healed
(Matthew 9:27–34)

As I went on from there, two blind men followed me, calling out, "Have mercy on us, Son of David."

When I got to the house, the blind men came to me. I said to them, "Do you believe I am able to restore your sight?"

They answered, "Yes, Lord."

So I touched their eyes as I said, "May it be done according to your faith."

Their eyes were opened, so I sternly warned them not to tell anyone about it. But they did just the opposite; they spread their story all over the area. As they were leaving, a dumb man possessed by a demon was brought to me. When the demon was cast out, the man spoke. The people were amazed, saying, "We never saw anything like this in Israel."

But the Pharisees repeated what they had said other times: "He casts out demons by the prince of demons."

Last Visit to Nazareth
(Matthew 13:54–58; Mark 6:1–6)

I returned to Nazareth with my disciples and on the Sabbath I taught in the synagogue. The people were astonished at my teaching. They said, "Where did he get all this wisdom? What great works he has done with his hands! Isn't he the carpenter— the son of Mary and the brother of James, Joseph, Judas and Simon? Don't we also have his sisters with us?"

In spite of the evidence, they could not accept who I was, so they were offended by me. I said to them, "A prophet receives honor everywhere except in his own hometown and amongst his own relatives." I couldn't do any significant miracles there, other than to lay hands on a few sick people who were healed. I was saddened by the extent of their unbelief. It amazed me.

(Matthew 9:35–38)

From Nazareth we went through many of the towns and villages, teaching in the synagogues and preaching the gospel of the kingdom. I healed every disease and physical deformity. As I saw the crowds everywhere I was moved to tears. They were sheep without a shepherd, aimless and helpless in the hands of those who only used them for their own purposes. I said to my disciples, "The harvest is plentiful but there are so few who care enough to labor. Pray, therefore, to the Lord of the harvest that he sends out laborers into this harvest."

The Twelve Sent Out
(Matthew 10:1, 5–42, 11:1; Mark 6:7–13; Luke 9:1–6)

I called my twelve disciples together and sent them out in pairs. I gave them power and authority over demons and to heal every disease and deformity. I gave them specific instructions: "Don't go to any of the towns of the Gentiles or the Samaritans. Stick with the lost sheep of Israel. Preach wherever you go, 'The kingdom of God is near.' Heal the sick, raise the dead, cleanse the lepers and cast out demons. You were given this power at no cost to you, so serve without pay. Travel light. Take nothing for your journey: no gold, silver or copper, no bread or backpack. Wear sandals and take no staff unless necessary. Don't even take two shirts.

"In whatever town or village you enter, stay with whoever is worthy. Stay in that same house until you leave. When you enter the home, speak peace upon it. If the home is worthy, your peace will remain, but if it is not, your peace will return to you. Wherever they will not receive you or listen to your words, shake the dust off your feet as you leave as a testimony against them. I solemnly affirm, it will be more tolerable for Sodom and Gomorrah on the Day of Judgment than for that town.

"Understand this, I am sending you out as sheep surrounded by wolves, so be wise as serpents and innocent as doves. Don't trust men, for they will turn you over to courts and beat you up in their synagogues. You will be dragged before governors and kings because you bear my name. You will testify in front of them and the nations as my ambassadors. When you are brought before them, don't worry about what you are going to say, for your Father will cause the Holy Spirit to speak through you.

"In days to come, a brother will turn in his own brother to be put to death, and a father, his child. Children will turn their parents over to the executioner. You will be hated because you belong to me and my name is your identity, but he who endures to the end will be saved. If they persecute you in one town, run to the next; I assure you, you will not get through all the towns of Israel before the Son of Man comes. A disciple is not greater than his teacher, nor a slave, his master. The most a disciple can be is to become like his teacher, or a slave, his master. If they call the master of the house the prince of demons, imagine what they will call the members of his household!

"Don't fear them, for all that is concealed will be brought out into the light and all that is hidden will become common knowledge. Whatever I tell you in the dark, tell it in the light. Whatever you hear whispered, shout out loud. Don't be afraid of those who can only kill the body but cannot kill the soul. You should fear the one who can destroy both body and soul in hell.

"Aren't two sparrows sold for a penny? Yet not one of them dies without your Father noticing it. Even the hairs of your head are numbered. Don't be afraid, then; you are far more valuable than many sparrows. Everyone who owns me before men I will also own before my Father in heaven. But whoever denies me before men I will also deny before my Father in heaven.

"Don't think I have come to bring peace on earth. My coming will not bring peace but a sword. My coming will pit a man against his father, a daughter against her mother and a daughter-in-law against her mother-in-law. A man's enemies will be members of his own house.

"He who loves father or mother more than he loves me is not worthy of me, and he who loves son or daughter more than he loves me is not worthy of me. He who does not take his cross and follow me is not worthy of me. He who pursues his own ideas of what he wants in life will lose my offer of eternal life. However, he who abandons his own ideas of what he wants in life and turns to serve me will find life both now and in the hereafter. Whoever accepts you as my follower accepts me also, and whoever accepts me also accepts the one who sent me. Whoever accepts a prophet because he is a prophet receives a prophet's reward, and whoever accepts a righteous man because he is righteous shall receive a righteous man's reward. Whoever gives even a cup of cold water to one of the least of my disciples because he is a disciple will not fail to receive his reward."

So the disciples went out through the villages preaching a gospel of repentance. They cast out many demons and healed the sick, anointing them with oil. I also went out teaching and preaching in the cities.

Death of John the Baptist
(Matthew 14:1–12; Mark 6:14–29; Luke 9:7–9)

Herod, the tetrarch, heard about my ministry. He was puzzled because some said John the Baptist had been raised from the dead. Others thought I was Elijah or one of the old prophets. Herod even said to some of his servants that John had been raised from the dead. Because of these rumors, he tried to see me.

John had recently been beheaded by Herod. It started when Herod put him in prison because he told Herod it was not legal to marry his brother's wife, Herodias. Herodias carried a grudge against John and would have killed him earlier, but Herod would not allow it. Herod feared John; he knew he was upright and holy, so he protected him. He could not understand John's message, yet he willingly listened to John.

Eventually Herodias got her opportunity. It was Herod's birthday and he threw a big banquet for the leading men of Galilee. Her daughter came in and danced, delighting Herod and his guests. Foolishly, Herod said to her, "I will give you whatever you wish, even half of the kingdom."

The girl went out and asked her mother what she should ask for. Instantly Herodias answered, "The head of John the Baptist." The girl returned immediately to the king.

"Give me the head of John the Baptist on a platter, right away."

The king was very disturbed, but because of his promise and the presence of his guests, he sent a soldier to look after her request. John was beheaded in prison. His head was handed to the girl on a platter, which she immediately took to her mother.

John's disciples heard what happened, so they came and took his body and laid it in a tomb. They reported the event to Jesus.

Feeding the Five Thousand
(Matthew 14:13–21; Mark 6: 30–44; Luke 9:10–17; John 6:1–14)

About this time the twelve returned, telling me all about what they had done and taught. I said, "Let us get away to a lonely place by ourselves to rest for a while." I said this because we were swamped with people coming and going endlessly. So we went away in a boat on the Sea of Galilee. We came on shore near the town of Bethsaida. The crowds found out where we were and followed around the lakeshore. Then we retreated into the hills, where I sat down with my disciples for a while. Looking up, I saw a large crowd approaching. Sadness swept over me, for no one cared for their plight. I was filled with compassion so I welcomed them. I healed their sick and taught them many things.

The day was wearing on, so my disciples came to me, saying, "This is a lonely place and it is getting late; it's time to send them away to buy food for themselves."

I replied, "You give them something to eat."

Philip said, "Two hundred days' wages wouldn't be enough to give them even a little bit each."

Andrew, Simon Peter's brother, came to me with a boy. "This lad has five barley loaves and two fish, but what use are they for so many?"

I said, "Bring them to me." We were in a nice grassy place so I instructed the disciples to have the people sit down in groups of about fifty. So they all sat down. I took the five loaves and two fish in my hands and, looking up to heaven, gave thanks for them. I began breaking them in pieces, giving them to my disciples to distribute. Everyone ate all they needed. When they were all fed, I told my disciples, "Pick up the left-over pieces. Don't waste anything." When they gathered them up, they had twelve baskets full. I fed about five thousand men plus women and children.

When the people realized the extent of the miracle they said, "This is surely the prophet who is coming into the world!" I realized they were all ready to come and take me by force to make me a king, so I immediately made my disciples get into the boat to head across the lake.

Walking on the Water
(Matthew 14:22–33; Mark 6:45–52; John 6:15–21)

As for myself, I escaped up into the hills to pray alone. A strong wind was blowing on the sea and my disciples were struggling to make headway against the waves as the wind was against them. I saw their problem, so I came out to them, walking on the water. By the time they saw me they had rowed about three or four miles. The sight of me only frightened them all the more because they thought they must be seeing a ghost.

When they cried out in terror, I immediately called to them, "It is I; don't be afraid."

Peter spoke up, "Since it's you, Lord, would you invite me to come to you on the water?"

I said, "Sure."

Peter stepped out of the boat and began walking toward me on the water. But it wasn't long before he looked at the big waves all around him and lost his courage, so he yelled, "Lord, save me!"

I immediately reached out my hand and caught him because he was sinking. I said to him, "How small is your faith. Why did you doubt?"

When we stepped into the boat, the wind quit and we came to the shore as planned. The disciples in the boat bowed in worship, saying, "You really are the Son of God."

Jesus Heals at Gennesaret
(Matthew 14:34–36; Mark 6:53–56)

We had now arrived at Gennesaret, so we got out of the boat. Many people recognized me, so they spread the word all over the region and brought the sick to me. Wherever I went, they laid the sick in the marketplaces. They knew that, even if they only touched the hem of my garment, they would be healed. As many as touched it were restored to health.

I Am the Bread of Life
(John 6:22–71)

The people I fed had returned to Capernaum, expecting to see me there. Boats had also gone out from Tiberias to the place where I fed them, but they didn't find me or my disciples there, so they returned to Capernaum. Eventually we made our way back to Capernaum as well.

The people asked me, "Teacher, when did you come back?"

I knew the thinking behind that question so I responded, "The truth is, you are searching for me because I filled you up with food. You are not seeking me because you saw the evidence of who I am. You are not interested in me for who I am but for what I can do for you. Don't just labor for food that only sustains this life for a little while; rather, labor for the food which endures, leading to eternal life. This is the food the Son of Man can give you because God, the Father, has put his seal of approval on him."

This intrigued them, so they asked me, "What do we have to do to be doing the work God wants?"

I replied, "This is the only work God wants of you: you must believe in the one who has been sent by him."

They came back with this question: "What great sign from heaven are you going to do so that we may believe in you? What are you going to perform? Our fathers ate manna in the wilderness, as it is written, 'He gave them bread from heaven to eat.'"[38]

I said, "I tell you the truth, it wasn't Moses who gave you bread from heaven. My Father gives you the true bread from heaven. The bread of God is that which comes down from heaven, giving life to the world."

They became more enthusiastic. "Lord, give us this bread always!"

They were not getting the point, so I continued, "I am the bread of life; whoever comes to me will never hunger and whoever believes in me will never thirst. I already said you do not believe in me even though you have seen me. All those given to me by my Father will come to me, and those who come to me I will never reject. I have not come down from heaven to do my own will. No! I have come to do the will of my Father who sent me. My Father who sent me has given me this mandate: I am to lose none of those he has chosen to give me; rather, I am to raise all of them up on the last day. This is what my Father has willed: everyone who sees the Son and believes in him shall have eternal life and I will raise each one up on the last day."

The people's enthusiasm now evaporated, for they realized I wasn't going to keep feeding them. They couldn't understand how I could be the bread which came down from heaven, so they murmured to one another, "Isn't this Jesus, the son of

---

[38] Psalm 78:24

Joseph? We know his father and mother. How can he say, 'I have come down from heaven'?"

I responded to them, "Don't complain to one another. No one can come to me unless my Father who sent me draws them. Then I will raise them up on the last day. The prophets wrote, 'And they shall all be taught by God.'[39] Everyone who has listened and applied teaching from my Father comes to me. I am not saying that anyone has seen the Father, for only the one who comes from God has ever seen him. This is the absolute truth; whoever believes has eternal life.

"Again, I say to you, I am the bread of life. Though your fathers ate the manna in the wilderness, they still died just the same as if they ate any other food. If you eat the bread that I am talking about, which comes down from heaven, you will never die." To further clarify what I meant, I touched the fingers of my right hand to my heart, saying, "I—the one who stands before you now—I am that living bread which came down from heaven; whoever eats this bread will live forever. The bread I give for the life of the world is my flesh."

The Jews looked at me in disbelief as they argued with one another, "How can this man give us his flesh to eat?"

So I waded in even further. "This is the absolute truth: unless you eat the flesh of the Son of Man and drink his blood, you do not have life in you. Whoever eats my flesh and drinks my blood has eternal life and I will raise them to life on the last day. My flesh is real food and my blood is real drink. Whoever keeps on eating my flesh and drinking my blood continues to live in unity with me and I with him. Just as the living Father sent me and I live in your presence because of my Father, likewise he who continues to eat of me will live because of me." Again, pointing to myself, I said, "This is the bread which came down from heaven; whoever eats this bread will live forever— no comparison to the manna—the fathers still died!"

---

[39] Isaiah 54:13

I said all this as I taught in the synagogue in Capernaum. Having heard this, many of my disciples said, "This is a difficult message; who can understand it?"

I realized they were struggling with what I said, so I addressed them personally, "Do you find this offensive? What if you saw the Son of Man ascending to where he came from?

"The life I am talking about is given by the Spirit. Flesh has no power to produce this kind of life. The words I have spoken are not about flesh but about spirit and spiritual life. Some of you struggle because you do not believe."

From the beginning, I knew who really believed and who did not. I also knew who was going to betray me, so I said, "That's why I told you that no one can come to me unless the Father grants it to them." After this many of my disciples walked away and no longer accompanied me.

So I turned to the twelve and asked, "Will you also go away?"

Simon Peter answered for them, "Lord, who else is there to go to? You have the message of eternal life. We now believe and have come to know that you are the Holy One of God."

I replied to them, "Didn't I choose all twelve of you, and even one of you is a devil?" Of course, I referred to Judas, the son of Simon Iscariot. He was the one of the twelve who would betray me.

Ceremonial Washing
(Matthew 15:1–20; Mark 7:1–23)

While I was in Galilee, a group of Pharisees came to me from Jerusalem. They noticed my disciples were eating without the ceremonial washing prescribed by the Jewish elders. The elders maintain endless ceremonial washings concerning cups and various pots as well as hand washing. They came to me, asking, "Why do your disciples not follow the tradition of the elders, instead eating with defiled hands?"

I answered them, "Isaiah did well when he prophesied about you hypocrites, saying, 'These people pay me lip-service, but their heart is entirely somewhere else. They make a great show of worshipping me, teaching man-made doctrines and human precepts.'[40] You promote your tangled web of tradition while rejecting the commandment of God. God gave Moses this command, 'Honor your father and mother. He who speaks evil of his father or mother must be put to death.'[41] But you say, 'If anyone tells his father or mother that he cannot help them because he has vowed his property to God, he can no longer do anything for his father or mother.' Thus, you violate the law of God."

I called the people to me and said to them, "Understand this. Nothing outside of you that you eat or drink can defile you, but the words that come out of you—these are what defile you."

Having said this, I left the people and went inside the house. My disciples came to me and said, "Are you aware the Pharisees were outraged by what you said?"

I replied, "Every plant not sown by my Father will be rooted up. Leave them alone; they are blind teachers. If one blind man tries to lead another blind man, they will both fall into the ditch."

Peter asked, "Would you explain the meaning of what you were teaching?"

I answered him, "You don't understand either? Don't you see that what you eat doesn't defile you because it does not enter the heart but only the stomach and then passes on? What comes out of your mouth is what defiles because your talk reveals what is in your heart. It is from the heart that all types of evil come: stealing, murder, adultery, greed, lying, filth, envy, slander, conceit and all kinds of selfishness. These are the things that defile a person. Eating with unwashed hands does not defile a person."

---

[40] Isaiah 29:13
[41] Exodus 20:12; Deuteronomy 5:16; Leviticus 20:9

Visit to Phoenicia
(Matthew 15:21–28; Mark 7:24–30)

I took my disciples and left Capernaum for the region of Tyre and Sidon. We entered a house in that area, trying our best to not be noticed. We didn't succeed, however, for no sooner had we arrived than a woman whose daughter was possessed by an unclean spirit came looking for me. She fell at my feet, crying out, "Have mercy on me, Lord, Son of David. My daughter is possessed by a demon."

Because she was a Syrophoenician, I did not even speak a word to her. But she persisted, calling out to my disciples. Finally they said to me, "Send her away! She's driving us crazy with her incessant begging."

I said to them, "I was sent only to the lost sheep of Israel."

With that, the woman fell at my feet again, imploring, "Lord, help me!"

It was then I spoke to her, "I must feed the children first; it isn't right to throw the children's food to the dogs before the children are all fed."

Her response amazed me: "Yes, Lord, that is true, but even the dogs eat the crumbs that the children drop under the table."

I could no longer deny her request, so I turned to her to say what I could rarely say to anyone in Israel, "Woman, you have incredible faith! Go home; the demon has left your daughter." She went home and found her daughter at peace, lying in her bed.

Journey through Decapolis
(Matthew 15:29–31; Mark 7:31–37)

We left the region of Tyre and Sidon, traveling east to Decapolis (The Ten Cities) on the east side of the Sea of Galilee. We went up into the hills, where we sat down for a time. Another large crowd gathered, bringing all kinds of handicapped people: the lame, blind and dumb, as well as those suffering from other sicknesses. They laid them at my feet. My heart ached for them so I healed them all.

They brought to me a man who was deaf with a speech impediment. I recognized this was a difficult case, so I took him aside from the crowd. I put my fingers in his ears, spat, and then touched his tongue. As I did this I sighed deeply and looked up to heaven, saying, "Ephatha," meaning, "Be opened." His ears were opened and his tongue released so that he spoke plainly. I told the man and those who brought him not to tell anyone. But it did no good. It seemed the more I said that, the more they told everyone.

When the crowd saw how the dumb spoke, the lame walked, the crippled became whole and the blind saw, they glorified my Father, the God of Israel. "He does everything well," they said, "He even makes the deaf hear and the dumb speak."

The Four Thousand Fed
(Matthew 15:32–39; Mark 8:1–10)

The crowd continued with us for some time. Finally, I called my disciples together, telling them, "My heart goes out to these people, for they have been with us three days now; they have run out of food so they are hungry. Many of them have come a long way. They could faint on the way home."

My disciples responded, "Where could we get enough bread out here in this wilderness to feed them all?"

I asked them what bread we had on hand. They replied, "Seven loaves and a few small fish." So I told all the people to sit down. Then I took the loaves and the fish and gave thanks for them. As I broke them, I handed the pieces to my disciples, who gave them out to the people. Everyone had enough to eat. In all, there were about 4,000 men besides women and children, and when they were done eating, my disciples collected up seven baskets full of the broken pieces that remained. I then sent the people away to their homes.

Pharisees and Sadducees want a Sign
(Matthew 16:1–4; Mark 8:10–13)

We immediately got into the boat and went south on the Sea of Galilee to the region of Dalmanutha (Magadan). Before we got far, a group of Pharisees and Sadducees met us. They demanded a spectacular sign from heaven to test me. My spirit was troubled, and I sighed deeply, saying, "Does this generation ever quit looking for a sign? When it is evening and the sky is red you say, 'It will be fair weather.' In the morning when the sky is red, you say, 'It will be a stormy day.' You can interpret what the day will be by looking at the sky, but you are blind to the meaning of the signs of the times. An evil and adulterous generation is always looking for a sign. I can assure you, no sign shall be given to this generation except the sign of the prophet Jonah."

I turned away from them as I gathered my disciples into the boat to go across the lake.

Leaven of the Pharisees
(Matthew 16:5–12; Mark 8:14–21)

While we were in the boat, I said to my disciples, "Be aware of the leaven of the Pharisees and Sadducees. Be wide awake so you aren't taken in by it or the leaven of Herod."

My disciples had forgotten to bring bread so there was only one loaf in the boat. They were so preoccupied by their oversight they thought I was speaking about bread, so they said to one another, "We didn't bring any bread."

Being aware of their concern, I continued, "Why are you discussing the fact you have no bread? Don't you understand? Are your eyes so blind and your ears so deaf that you don't remember? When I broke the five loaves for 5,000, how many baskets full did you collect?"

They said, "Twelve."

"And when I broke the seven loaves for the 4,000, how many baskets did you collect?"

They said, "Seven."

"Then what made you think I was speaking about the lack of bread? I was speaking of the leaven of the Pharisees and Sadducees." Then they understood I was warning them about the teaching of the Pharisees and Sadducees.

Blind Man of Bethsaida
(Mark 8:22–26)

We came ashore at Bethsaida at the north end of the Sea of Galilee. Some people brought a blind man to me, begging me to heal him. Knowing what would happen if I healed him right there, I took him by the hand and led him out of town. I spat on his eyes and laid my hands on him. Then I asked, "Can you see anything?"

He looked around and said, "I see men, but they look like trees walking around." So I laid my hands on his eyes again.

When he looked this time, his vision cleared up and he could see perfectly. I sent him home, saying, "Go straight home; don't even enter the village."

Peter's Confession
(Matthew 16:13–20; Mark 8:27–30; Luke 9:18–21)

We soon left Bethsaida and travelled north to the area of Caesarea Philippi. We ministered in the villages of that area. One day as we were alone and I was praying, I turned to my disciples and asked them, "Who do the people say that I am?"

They answered, "Some say John the Baptist; others say Elijah, even Jeremiah. Still others say that one of the old prophets has risen."

Then I said to them, "But who do you say that I am?"

Simon Peter spoke up, "You are the Christ, the Son of the living God."

I replied to him, "Blest are you, Simon Bar-Jona! Flesh and blood hasn't revealed this to you; my Father in heaven has himself directly revealed this to you. I say to you, you are Peter, and on this rock I will build my church. The powers of hell will not prevail against it. I will give you the keys to the kingdom of

God; whatever you bind on earth will be bound in heaven and whatever you release on earth will be released in heaven." Then I strictly commanded my disciples to not tell anyone that I was the Christ.

Death and Resurrection Predicted
(Matthew 16:21–23; Mark 8:31–33; Luke 9:22)

At this time, I began telling my disciples what lay ahead of me. I told them I had to go to Jerusalem, where I would suffer many things. I would be rejected by the elders, the chief priests and the scribes. I would be killed, but on the third day I would rise again. This was more than Peter could handle so he came up to me, countering what I had said. He spoke strongly, "God forbid, Lord! This can't ever happen to you!"

I instantly rebuked him in no uncertain terms, "Get out of here, Satan! You are a stumbling-block to me. You are not on God's side; you are expressing the reasoning of men."

The Cost of Discipleship
(Matthew 16:24–28; Mark 8:34–9:1; Luke 9:23–27)

Later, I spoke to my disciples and to the crowd that had gathered, "If any man chooses to follow me, he must abandon his own plans for his life, take up his cross daily and follow me. For whoever chooses his own way in this life will lose everything in the end, including eternal life. But whoever puts his life on the line for my sake and the sake of the good news will lose nothing in this life or in the life to come. What good is it if a man gains the entire world only to lose life eternal and what might have been in this life. For what can a man give to regain his life?

"Whoever is ashamed of me and my words in this adulterous and sinful generation will find that I, the Son of Man, will also be ashamed of them. For I will return in the splendor of my Father with the holy angels and will repay every man for what he has done. I solemnly say to you, there are some standing here who will see the kingdom of God come in power before they experience death."

The Transfiguration
(Matthew 17:1–13; Mark 9:2–13; Luke 9:28–36)

About a week later, I took Peter, James and John with me up a high mountain. There was no one else with us. As we were praying, my entire appearance was changed. My face shined like the sun and my clothes became dazzling white. Then Moses and Elijah appeared and talked to me about my leaving earth, which was to take place at Jerusalem. The three disciples were very tired, but they were awake enough to see my glory and the two men standing with me. They were overcome by what they saw.

Peter, though filled with fear, felt he had to say something, so he blurted out, "Master, it is good that we are here. Let's make three tents: one for you, one for Moses and one for Elijah." He hardly knew what he said. By this time Moses and Elijah had left.

Suddenly a bright cloud overshadowed us and a voice spoke from the cloud, "This is my beloved Son, who brings me great joy. Listen to him!"

When the disciples heard this, they fell on their faces, completely awestruck. I walked over to them and touched them, saying, "You can get up; don't be afraid." They rubbed their eyes and, looking around, saw that everything was back to normal. I was standing there alone, as before.

As we were coming down the mountain, I commanded them not to tell anyone what they had seen until after I was raised from the dead. They did as I told them, keeping everything to themselves. They still didn't know what the rising from the dead meant.

As we went along, the disciples asked me, "Why do the scribes say that Elijah must come first?"[42] I replied, "Elijah does come first to restore all things. Why is it written that the Son of

---

[42] Malachi 4:5–6

Man will suffer many things and be rejected?[43] I tell you the truth, Elijah has come and they treated him just as it suited them. In the same way, I will suffer in their hands." Then my disciples understood I was speaking of John the Baptist.

Demon-Possessed Boy Healed
(Matthew 17:14–21; Mark 9:14–29; Luke 9:37–43)

The next day when we had come down from the mountain, we saw the other disciples with a large crowd gathered around them. Some scribes were arguing with them. When the crowd saw me they ran up to me. I asked what all the discussion was about. A man from the crowd came up to me. He explained, "Teacher, I brought my mute son to you because he has a spirit that seizes him. It throws him on the ground and he foams at the mouth. He grinds his teeth and stiffens up. I asked your disciples to cast it out but they couldn't."

I replied, "Oh, you unbelieving and obstinate generation, how long must I stay with you? How long do I have to put up with this? Bring the boy to me."

As soon as the spirit saw me, it convulsed the boy so that he fell on the ground, rolling around and foaming at the mouth. I asked his father, "How long has he been like this?"

"From childhood," he said, "and he has often been thrown into fire or water. If you can do anything, have pity on us and help us."

"If I can? All things are possible to those who believe."

Immediately the father cried out, "I believe, help my unbelief!"

I saw the crowd was rushing toward us, so I commanded the unclean spirit, "You dumb and deaf spirit, come out of him at once and never enter him again." The spirit shrieked and threw the boy violently to the ground.

The boy looked like he was dead. Some even said, "He is dead." I took him by the hand and pulled him up on his feet. The

---

[43] Psalm 22;6–7; Isaiah 50:3; 53:3

boy was fine, so I gave him back to his father. Everyone was astonished at the greatness of God.

After I went home, the disciples asked me privately, "Why couldn't we cast it out?"

I responded, "Because of your meager faith. I tell you, if you had the faith of a grain of mustard seed, you could say to this mountain, 'Move over there,' and it would move. Nothing would be impossible for you."

Through Galilee to Capernaum
(Matthew 17:22–23; Mark 9:30–32; Luke 9:44–45)

To get away from the crowds, I took my disciples with me through quiet areas of Galilee so I could teach them. I said, "I will be delivered to men who will kill me. After three days I will rise from the dead." However, the truth was hidden from them so they couldn't understand. This message greatly disturbed them, but they were afraid to ask what I meant. We returned to Capernaum after this time.

The Temple Tax
(Matthew 17:24–27)

When we arrived in Capernaum, those who collected the half-shekel temple tax came up to Peter and asked him, "Doesn't your teacher pay the temple tax?"

Peter said, "Yes, he does."

When we returned to the house, I spoke to Peter, "What do you think, Simon? Who do human kings collect tribute from: their own sons or other people?"

Peter answered, "From others."

"That means, then, that the sons go free." I continued, "So as not to offend them, go to the sea and throw out a hook; take the first fish you catch and open its mouth. You will find a shekel. Take it to them for me and for yourself."

The Greatest in the Kingdom
(Matthew 18:1–14; Mark 9:33–50; Luke 9:46–51; 17:1–2)

When we were in the house, the disciples started arguing among themselves about who was the greatest. I knew in my heart what the discussion was about, but I asked them, "What were you discussing along the way?" There was total silence! So I sat down with them around me. "If anyone wants to be first, he must choose to be last, to be servant of everyone else." I then called a small child and put him in the middle of our circle. "Unless you abandon your status-seeking and become like little children, you will never enter the kingdom of God." Gesturing toward the little boy, I continued, "Whoever humbles himself like this child will be the greatest in the kingdom of God."

I then picked up the little boy and held him in my arms. I went on. "Whoever receives a child like this in my name receives me, and whoever receives me receives my Father who sent me. The one who is least among you all is truly great."

John spoke up, "Master, we saw a man casting out demons in your name. We told him to stop because he was not following with us."

I said to John, "Don't stop him, for anyone who does miracles in my name will not soon speak evil of me. Whoever is not against us is for us; he is on our side. I solemnly say to you, whoever gives you even a cup of water to drink because you bear my name will never go unrewarded."

Turning their attention again to the child in my arms, I said, "Whoever causes one of these little ones who believe in me to sin, he would have been better off if he had been thrown into the depths of the sea and drowned with a great millstone around his neck. A curse is on the world because of temptations to sin! Temptations will inevitably come, but cursed is the one who brings them. If your hand or foot causes you to sin, cut it off and throw it away. It is better to enter heaven dismembered than to spend eternity with both hands or feet in the unending fires of hell. If your eye causes you to sin, pluck it out and throw it away. It is better to enter the kingdom of God with one eye than to have two eyes in the pit of hell. There the worm doesn't die and the fire never goes out. Salt is good, but if the salt has become tasteless what can restore it? Be salty in yourselves and live at peace with one another.

"Never despise one of these little ones. I solemnly say to you that their angels always look into the face of my Father in heaven. What do you think? When a man has a hundred sheep and he finds one has strayed off, doesn't he leave the ninety-nine and go searching for the missing one? Then, when he finds it, doesn't he rejoice more over the one he brought back than all the others that were safe in the fold? In the same way, it is not the will of my Father in heaven that even one of these little ones should perish."

Forgiving Your Brother
(Matthew 18:15–35)

"If your brother sins against you, don't carry a grudge; rather go and tell him how he has hurt you. Don't bring anyone else into the issue at this point; it is just between the two of you. If he listens to you, you have restored your brother.

"If he does not listen, then take one or two others with you as witnesses so that all that is said may be confirmed. If he refuses to listen to them, it is time to take it to the church. If he will not even listen to the church, then consider him cut off from fellowship with you.

"I tell you, whatever you bind on earth will be bound in heaven, and whatever you release on earth will be released in heaven. Let me say this: if two of you agree on earth about anything they ask for, my Father in heaven will do it for you, because wherever two or three gather in my name, I am right there in the middle with them."

Peter asked, "Lord, how often should I forgive my brother if he keeps sinning against me? Up to seven times?"

I replied, "Forget seven times; forgive seventy times seven if necessary.

"The kingdom of God can be compared to a king who wanted to settle accounts with his servants. He added up the debts and found one who owed him $10,000,000.[44] So the king ordered him, his wife and children and all his possessions to be sold because he could not pay. The servant came and fell at his feet. He begged the king, 'Lord, have patience with me and I will pay you everything.' The king felt sorry for him so he released him and forgave the entire debt.

"But as soon as the servant left the palace, he came upon a fellow servant who owed him twenty dollars.[45] He seized him by the throat, demanding, 'Pay me what you owe!' His fellow servant fell down and begged, 'Have patience with me and I will pay you.' He refused. Instead he put his fellow servant in prison till he should pay the twenty dollars. The other servants were greatly upset when they saw what he did. They went and reported to the king all that he did. The king summoned the man before him and said, 'You wicked servant! I forgave you that huge debt because you begged me. Shouldn't you have mercy on your fellow servant like I had on you?' The king was very angry, so he sent him to jail until he paid the entire debt. This is what my heavenly Father will do to every one of you who refuses to forgive your brother from your heart."

Attending the Festival of Tents
(Matthew 8:19–22; Luke 9:51–62; John 7:1–53)

I continued on in Galilee for some time, going from town to town. I stayed out of Judea because the Jewish leaders there were plotting to kill me. Eventually fall was upon us, the time for the festival of tents. My brothers urged me to go to Judea for the celebration. Even they did not believe, so they made fun of me: "You won't become famous going through the villages of Galilee! You need to go to Judea where the action is. If you are doing all these wonderful miracles, let the world see what you can do!"

---

[44] 10,000 talents@$1000 each.

[45] 100 denarii @ twenty cents each.

Deeply hurt by their mockery, I replied, "It isn't time for me yet, but you can go any time. The world doesn't hate you because you fit right in. The world hates me because I confront all the sin and evil. Go to the feast yourselves; it's not the time for me." My brothers went up but I stayed in Galilee for a little longer. After the crowds had gone, I set out to go quietly with my disciples.

(Luke 9:51–56)

I sent messengers ahead of me to prepare for my coming. They entered a Samaritan village, but they refused to have me come because they realized I was on the way to Jerusalem.

When James and John heard this, they said to me, "Lord, do you want us to command fire to come down from heaven and burn them up?"

I instantly turned to them and rebuked them, saying, "You don't know what kind of spirit you are tuned into. The Son of Man did not come into the world to destroy people's lives but to save them." We carried on to another village.

(Matthew 8:19–22; Luke 9:57–62)

As we were going along the road, a scribe came up to me. "Teacher, I will follow you wherever you go."

I warned him, "Foxes have dens and the birds have nests, but the Son of Man doesn't even own a pillow to lay his head on."

I turned to another with an invitation, "Follow me."

But he said, "Lord, allow me to first bury my father."

I replied, "Let the dead bury their own dead, but you go and tell the good news about the kingdom of God."

A third person said, "I will follow you, Lord, but first let me say goodbye to those at home."

I told him, "No one who puts his hands on the plow but keeps looking back is fit for the kingdom of God."

(John 7:11–53)

Meanwhile, the seven-day feast had begun in Jerusalem. The Jews were looking for me.

"Where is he?" they asked. Between themselves many expressed different views of me. "He is a good man," some said. Others said, "No! He is leading the people astray." None spoke of me publicly because they feared the Jewish leaders.

At about the middle of the feast, I arrived and went into the temple and began to teach. Many of the Jews were amazed.

"How come this man knows all this when he has never studied with the teachers?"

I knew what they were saying, so I answered them, "My teaching does not come from me; it comes from him who sent me. If anyone determines to do the will of him who sent me, he will know if my teaching comes from God or if it just comes from me. Whoever speaks on his own authority tries to glorify himself. Whoever sets out to bring glory to the one who sent him tells the truth. He does not lie.

"You all know Moses gave you the Law, yet not one of you obeys the Law. On what grounds, then, are you trying to kill me?"

The people answered me, "You are out of your mind—you must be possessed by a demon! Who is trying to kill you?"

I continued, "You marveled when I healed a man, yet you hate me because I did it on the Sabbath. Moses commanded you to circumcise sons on the eighth day just as the fathers did all the way back to Abraham. If the eighth day falls on the Sabbath, you circumcise a boy as Moses commanded. In so doing you are working on the Sabbath. Why, then, are you angry with me for healing a man's body on the Sabbath? Do not judge by what things look like—make a fair judgment."

Hearing this, some in Jerusalem said, "Isn't this the man they want to kill? How come he is speaking outright in the temple and no one says anything? Can it be that the authorities really know this is the Christ? On the other hand, we know where this man comes from; when the Christ appears, no one will know where he is from."

I continued teaching in the temple, speaking loudly so they could all hear. "So you know me and you know where I come from. But my coming is not my own doing; the one who sent me is Truth. He cannot lie. You do not know him. I do know him, for I come from him and he sent me."

Some tried to arrest me, yet not a hand was laid on me. That was because my ministry was not yet done. The many people who now believed in me said to one another, "When the Christ does come, can he do more signs than this man has done?"

The Pharisees heard what the crowd was saying, so they sent officers to arrest me. I continued teaching: "I shall only be with you a little longer. Then I shall return to the one who sent me. You will look all over but you will not find me because I will be where you cannot come."

The Jews became even more mystified. "Where does this man plan to go so that we will not be able to find him? Does he intend to teach the Jews who are scattered among the Greeks? Maybe he plans to teach the Greeks. How can he say there is a place he can go where we cannot come and so not be able to find him?"

On the last day of the feast, the most important day, I stood up again to proclaim: "If anyone is thirsty, let him come to me and drink. He who believes in me, out of his being shall flow rivers of living water, as the Scripture has said." (I was not talking about actual water but about the Holy Spirit, which those who believed in me would receive after my resurrection.)

After hearing my proclamation, the people continued their discussion among themselves. "This really is the prophet," said some. Others said, "This is the Christ." Others doubted, "Can the Christ come from Galilee? Doesn't Scripture say Christ is a descendant of David and comes from Bethlehem, David's hometown?" There was a division of opinion among the people. Some even wanted to arrest me, but no one laid hands on me.

Eventually the officers sent by the chief priests and Pharisees returned. "Why didn't you bring him?" they asked.

Having been moved, the officers replied, "No man has ever spoken like this man!"

The angry Pharisees belittled them: "Have you fallen for this fellow also? Haven't you noticed that none of the authorities believe in him? Of course, we Pharisees who interpret the Law are not deceived by his talk. As for this ignorant crowd who don't even know the Law, their gullible opinions don't count anyhow; they are already condemned."

Standing among them was Nicodemus, the Pharisee who had met with me before this. He spoke up, "Does our Law condemn a man without allowing him to testify in a court so that a proper judgment can be brought down?"

His fellow Pharisees now turned on him, "Are you from Galilee as well? You should know. Search all you like; you won't find any prediction of a prophet coming from Galilee." With that, the Pharisees dispersed.

The Adulterous Woman
*(John 8:1–11 *This passage is not in the older manuscripts of John)*

I had gone to the Mount of Olives in the evening, but I returned to the temple early in the morning. The people came to me in large numbers so I sat down and taught them. The scribes and Pharisees arrived with a woman caught in adultery. They pushed her out in the middle as "Exhibit A" for the accusation they were forming. They then turned and addressed me: "Teacher, this woman was caught in the very act of adultery. The law of Moses commanded us to stone her. What do you say?"

I knew this was a set-up, so I didn't answer right away. I bent down and wrote on the ground with my finger. The men continued to demand an answer, so I stood up and said, "Let him who has never sinned throw the first stone." Then I bent down again and continued writing on the ground. When they heard what I said, they started leaving, the oldest first.

Soon I was left with only the woman standing before me. I stood up and asked her, "Has no one condemned you?"

"No one, Lord," she answered.

So I said to her, "Neither do I; go your way and sin no more."

The Light of the World
(John 8:12–59)

After the woman left, a crowd of onlookers stood around me. I said, "I am the light of the world. Anyone who follows me will be able to see where to go. You will not be led down the wrong path by the lies the people of the world believe. I will show you the truth that leads to real life."

Some Pharisees didn't believe me. They thought they already had all the truth. "You are making claims for yourself that are not true," they said.

I answered them, "Even though I speak about myself, what I say is true because I know where I came from and I know where I am going. You do not know where I came from or where I am going. To you, I look like any other person. You are judging me based on your limited knowledge. I am not judging anyone, but if I did, it would be true, for I am not alone. The one who sent me knows the truth as I do. What I tell you about myself is the same as what my Father knows is true about me."

They said to me, "Where is your Father?"

I answered, "You don't know me, which proves that you don't know my Father either. If you knew me, you wouldn't be asking that question. You would already know my Father as well."

I spoke these words in the treasury as I taught in the temple. Even though the authorities were out to get me, no one arrested me because it was not yet my time.

(John 8:21–30)

When I resumed teaching, I said to them, "I will soon go away and you will look for me, but you will die in your sin. You cannot come where I am going."

The Jews questioned among themselves, "Is he going to kill himself? How else can he go where we cannot come?"

I explained further, "You are from below; I am from above. You belong to this world; I do not belong to this world. I already warned you, you will die with your sin still unforgiven. This is certain unless you believe that I am the Christ."

They responded, "Just who are you, anyway?"

I replied, "Why do I even talk to you at all? I am what I told you all along. I have a lot more to say about you and much to condemn. The one who sent me is truthful and I only tell the world what I hear from him." They didn't understand that I was speaking about the Father, so I continued, "When you lift up the Son of Man, you will know who I am. You will also understand that I never do or say anything that originates with me. All that I speak, the Father taught me. I have not been left here on my own; he who sent me is always with me. He stays with me because I always do what pleases him."

As I was speaking, many came to believe in me.

(John 8:31–59)

I said to the Jews who believed in me, "If you live in obedience to what I teach, you will indeed be my disciples. You will know the truth, and the truth will set you free."

This ruffled their feathers, so they adamantly said, "What do you mean, 'You will be set free'? We are children of Abraham and have never been slaves of anyone. How can you say that?"

I explained, "This is a central truth: whoever lives in sin has become a slave of sin. A slave is only in a house for a while; the Son is a permanent resident. So if the Son grants you freedom, you really will be free.

"I know you are descendants of Abraham, yet you try to kill me. That's because my teaching finds no place to lodge in you. What I speak about, I have seen in my Father's presence. You do what you have learned from your father."

Their quick response was expected: "Abraham is our father!"

My response became more direct: "If you are Abraham's children, you would be doing what Abraham did. As it is, you want to kill me because I have told you the truth. I received this truth from God. Abraham never rejected the truth. You are doing what your actual father did."

They now made the ultimate claim. "We are not illegitimate children. We have only one Father: God himself."

I replied, "If God were your Father, you would love me, because I came here from God. It was not my own plan; he sent me to you. Do you know why you cannot understand what I say? I will tell you—it's because you can't stand to hear what I teach. You are children of your father, the devil, and you only do what he wants. He was a murderer right from the start. He has nothing in common with truth because there is absolutely no truth in him. It is his nature to pour out lies, for he is the father of lies. He cannot do anything else. That's why, when I tell you the truth, you refuse to believe me. Who here can truthfully convict me of sin? Since I am telling the truth, why don't you believe me? Those who are children of God naturally hear the words of God. You don't hear the words of God, which proves you are not children of God."

The Jews were outraged. "Weren't we right when we said you were a Samaritan controlled by a demon?"

I answered "I do not have a demon. I am honoring my Father but you are dishonoring me. I am not looking to receive honor myself. There is one who honors me, and he will be the judge. I solemnly tell you, if anyone obeys my teaching, he will never see death."

The Jews pressed in. "Now we know you have a demon! Abraham and the prophets all died, and now you say, 'If anyone obeys my teaching he will never see death.' Are you greater than Abraham and the prophets who died? Who do you claim to be?"

I answered them, "If I set out alone to honor myself, my honoring would mean nothing. But I am not alone; it is my Father who honors me. He is the one you claim is your God. Your problem is that you don't know him. I do know him. I cannot say I do not know him because then I would be a liar like you. And since I do know him I obey his word. Your ancestor, Abraham was excited at the hope of seeing my day. He has seen it and is glad."

The Jews stared in disbelief. "You claim you have seen Abraham? You aren't even fifty years old!"

I stated, "This is the absolute truth: before Abraham existed, I AM."[46] They picked up stones to throw at me, but I hid myself and left the temple.

The Man Born Blind
(John 9:1–41)

As we were walking along, I saw a man who had been blind all his life. My disciples noticed him too, so they asked me, "Teacher, is this man blind because of his own sin or the sin of his parents?"

I responded, "His blindness has nothing to do with sin—neither his own nor that of his parents. God has allowed this so that his power will become evident in this man's life. We must do God's work while we have the light of day; night will come soon enough when no one can work. As long as I am here in the world, I am the light of the world."

Having said this, I spat on the ground and made some mud. I then smeared it on the man's eyes. I said to him, "Go and wash in the pool of Siloam." Without hesitation, he found his way to Siloam and washed his eyes. He came bouncing back, seeing everything for the very first time.

The neighbors couldn't help but notice him. They asked, "Isn't this the man who always sat and begged?" Some answered, "That's him all right." Others said, "It can't be, but he is like him."

They gathered around him. He confirmed, "I am the blind beggar."

"How come you can see now?"

"The man called Jesus put mud on my eyes, telling me to go and wash in Siloam. So I did, and now I can see."

The neighbors demanded, "Where is he?"

"I don't know," he responded.

No one shared his joy. Instead they only saw him as a problem, because it was the Sabbath day. So they took him to the

---

[46] Exodus 3:14

Pharisees. He was certainly a problem to them, so they asked him how he got his sight. He told the simple story, "Jesus put clay on my eyes, I washed, and now I can see."

The Pharisees were divided. Some said, "This man cannot be from God because he doesn't keep the Sabbath." But others said, "How can a man who is a sinner do such miracles?"

They turned to the blind man again, "What have you to say, since he opened your eyes?"

He answered, "He is a prophet!"

The Jews didn't believe he had been born blind so they called his parents. "Is this your son who was born blind? If he was, how come he can now see?"

His parents dodged the question. "We know this is our son who was born blind, but how he received his sight, we don't know. Neither do we know who opened his eyes. Why don't you ask him? He's old enough to speak for himself." They said this because the Jews had already decided that if anyone admitted they believed I was the Christ, they would be put out of the synagogue.

Again, the Pharisees called the once-blind man to them. This time they spoke as those in authority, "Give God the praise; we know this man is a sinner!"

The man responded, "I don't know whether he is a sinner or not, but this one thing I do know: once I was blind, but now I can see."

They pressed him further, "What did he do? How did he open your eyes?"

The formerly blind man was tired of this game so he fired back, "I have told you already and you didn't listen. Why do you want it all over again? Do you want to become his disciples?"

The Pharisees were infuriated, so they pulled rank. "You are his disciple, but WE are disciples of Moses. WE know God spoke to Moses. As for this guy, we don't even know his origin."

The formerly blind man read them like a book. He went on the offensive with inescapable logic: "This is amazing! You just admitted you don't know where he came from, a man who opened my eyes. Everyone knows God doesn't listen to sinners, but God always listens to those who worship him and do his will. Ever since the beginning of the world has anyone heard of someone opening the eyes of a man born blind? Unless God sent this man, he couldn't do anything."

The Pharisees were stumped so they attacked the man. "You were born in utter depravity and you dare to try to teach us?" In their rage, they threw him out.

I heard he had been thrown out of the synagogue, so I went to comfort him. "Do you believe in the Son of Man?"

He replied, "Sir, who is he? Tell me so I can believe in him."

"You have already seen him; he is the one who is speaking to you right now."

He immediately fell at my feet and worshipped, saying, "Lord, I believe!"

I spoke further, "My coming into this world has brought judgment. To those who could not see, I have brought vision; to those who claim to see, I have increased their blindness."

Some Pharisees who were sitting there heard what I said. They asked, "Are we also blind?"

I answered them, "If you were blind, you would not be guilty. But you claim you can see, so you are still guilty."

The Good Shepherd
(John 10:1–21)

After speaking to the man healed of blindness, I began to teach a group that gathered around me. "I assure you, anyone who tries to get into the sheepfold by clambering over the wall instead of using the door is a thief and a robber. The shepherd always comes in by the door. After the gatekeeper lets him in, the shepherd calls out to his own sheep by name. They all come to him because they know his voice. He then leads them out to pasture as they follow along. No stranger could trick them even if he knew their names. As soon as he opened his mouth, they would all run away from him, because they don't recognize the voices of strangers."

I told this story to those around me, but they had no idea what I meant by it, so I explained further. "I assure you, I am the door to the sheepfold. All those who came before me were thieves and robbers. My sheep didn't listen to them. Because I am the door, all those who come into the fold by me will be secure. They will freely go in and out and find pasture. The only reason the thief comes is to steal. He kills and destroys; I give them abundant life. I am the good shepherd, the only one who lays down his life for the sheep.

"The farm hand who doesn't own the sheep is not the shepherd. When he sees a wolf coming, he runs off to save his own skin. The wolf carries sheep off and the rest scatter. The hired man doesn't care one bit about the sheep. But I am the good shepherd. I know all my own sheep and they all know me. This relationship is like the one between my Father and I: my Father knows me and I know my Father. Unlike the hired man, I willingly lay down my life for the sake of the sheep.

"I have other sheep that are not part of this fold. I must bring them as well. They, too, will recognize my voice, so there will be one flock led by one shepherd. My Father loves me because I lay down my life, and I will take it again. No one has the power to take it from me; I voluntarily lay it down of my own free will. I have the authority to lay my life down, and I have the power to take it back again. I have been given this mandate by my Father."

Again, the Jews were divided about me when they heard these words. Some said, "This man is crazy; he's controlled by a demon! Why does anyone listen to him?" but others said, "A demon-controlled man doesn't speak like this. Can a demon open a blind man's eyes?"

The Seventy Sent Out
(Matthew 11:20–24; Luke 10:1–16)

After the Festival of Tents, I chose seventy more disciples to go ahead of me in pairs. They went into every town where I was going to come. I said to them, "There is a great harvest, but there aren't many to gather it. So pray to the Lord of the harvest to raise up laborers to help bring in the crop." I went on to instruct them. "Go on your way. You are like a flock of lambs being sent into a pack of wolves. Don't carry any money or bag, not even spare sandals. Don't stop to talk to anyone along the road.

"Whenever you go into a house, immediately say, 'Peace be upon this house.' If there is a man of peace there, your peace will stay with him. If there isn't, your peace will return to you. In any town, stay in the same house; don't go from house to house. Eat and drink whatever they serve. The laborer deserves his wages.

"When you come to a town and they accept you, eat what they offer you. Heal the sick that are there and tell them, 'The kingdom of God has come near.' If a town does not receive you, go into the streets and say, 'We wipe off against you even the dust from your town that clings to our feet. But know this, the kingdom of God has come near you.' I tell you, Sodom will do better at the judgment than that town."

I then began to speak against the cities where most of my miracles had been done. "You are cursed, Chorazin; you are cursed, Bethsaida! If the powerful miracles done in you were done in Tyre and Sidon, they would have long since repented, wearing sackcloth and sitting with ashes on their heads. Tyre and Sidon will receive better treatment on judgment day than you will. And as for you, Capernaum, do you expect to be raised up to heaven? No! You will be brought down to hell. If Sodom had seen the powerful miracles done in your town, it would still exist to this day. I assure you, Sodom will fare better at the judgment than you will. Whoever hears you, hears me, and whoever rejects you, rejects me. Whoever rejects me, rejects the one who sent me."

The Good Samaritan
(Luke 10:25–37)

One day a lawyer stood up to question me. "Teacher, what do I have to do to gain eternal life?"

I replied, "What do you find in the Law? What is your take on it?"

He answered, "You shall love the Lord your God with all your heart, with all your soul, with all your strength, and with all your mind; and love your neighbor as you love yourself."[47]

"You have answered correctly," I told him. "Continue doing that and you will live."

Seeking further clarification, he asked, "Who is my neighbor?"

I answered with a story:

"A man was on his way down to Jericho from Jerusalem when he was attacked by thieves. They stole everything, including his clothes, beat him up and left him half dead beside the road. A priest happened to come by. When he saw the man, he purposely went by on the other side of the road. Later, a Levite came by and did the same thing. Eventually a Samaritan came along. When he saw the poor man, his heart went out to him so he stopped. He poured on oil and wine and bandaged his wounds. He lifted the man up on his donkey and took him into the next inn. He took care of him until the next day when he had to leave. He gave the innkeeper two silver coins, saying, 'Look after him. If you spend more than this, I will repay you when I come back.' Of the three men, which one acted as a neighbor to the injured man?"

The lawyer replied, "The one who was merciful to him."

I said to him. "Right. Now you go and do the same."

Visiting Martha and Mary
(Luke 10:38–42)

As we went along, we came to a village where a woman named Martha welcomed us into her home. She had a sister, Mary, who loved to sit at my feet soaking up everything I said. But Martha was bustling around preparing a feast for us all. Her sister's inactivity greatly upset her, so she finally came to me and

---

[47] Deuteronomy 6:5

said, "Lord, doesn't it bother you that Mary sits there doing nothing while I do all the work? Tell her to come and help me."

I turned to Martha, and knowing her good heart but seeing her troubled face, I gently said to her, "Martha, Martha, you lay on yourself so much more than is ever necessary. In all your busyness, I don't even get to visit with you. Mary has understood all that my presence means; she has chosen the better part and it shall not be taken away from her."

About Prayer
(Luke 11:1–13)

One day I was praying, and when I finished, one of my disciples asked me, "Lord, would you teach us to pray as John taught his disciples?"

I said to them, "Pray this way: 'Father, may your name be honored; may your kingdom come. Give us bread for each day and forgive our sins in the same way we forgive those who have betrayed our trust. Don't let us be led into temptation.'"

I continued on, "Who hasn't at some point had to go to a friend at night, explaining, 'Can you loan me three loaves? A friend has arrived and I have nothing to feed him.' On your first request he will call out, 'No way, we are all in bed here. How can you expect me to get up and disturb my children to give you bread at this hour?' I assure you, his friendship will not be enough to get him out of his warm bed for you, but your persistence will get him out to meet your need.

"If a friend will do that, think what your heavenly Father will do. So ask, and you will receive; search, and you will discover; knock, and the door will be opened. When a child asks for a fish, what father would give him a snake? Who would give his child a scorpion when he asks for an egg? If even you who are evil know how to give good things to your children, never doubt how willingly your heavenly Father will give the Holy Spirit to those who ask him."

No Neutral Ground
(Luke 11:14–36)

I was casting a mute spirit out of a man as a crowd watched. When the spirit left, the dumb man spoke and everyone was amazed. But some of them claimed, "He casts demons out by the power of Satan, the prince of demons." Others kept badgering me for a spectacular sign to prove who I really was.

I knew what their thinking was behind all this, so I said to them, "If Satan is attacking his own demons, how long can his kingdom go on this way? You say I am casting out demons by the power of Satan. If that is what I am doing, then by what power do your sons cast them out? They will be your judges. But if I am casting out demons by the finger of God, then the kingdom of God has come into your presence.

"When a powerful man, fully armed, guards his place, his property is secure. But if an even stronger man attacks and overpowers him, he carts off all his goods, even stripping off the armor he trusted in. There is no neutral ground in this spiritual battle; whoever does not stand with me is against me. Whoever does not join me in the work is tearing it down.

"When an unclean spirit goes out of a man, the spirit travels through desert places trying to find rest. When it doesn't find anything, it says to itself, 'I'm going back to the house I came from.' When it returns and finds it clean and in order, it finds seven more spirits even more wicked than itself. They all move in, and the final state of the man is much worse than it was before."

While I was teaching, a woman spoke up loudly, "Blest is the woman who gave birth to you and nursed you!"

But I replied, "Even more blest are those who listen to the word of God and carry it out."

As the crowds were getting larger, I went on to say, "You are seeking a sign. You do this because this generation is an evil generation. You will not be given a sign except the sign of Jonah. Just as Jonah became a sign to the city of Ninevah, the Son of Man will be a sign to this generation.

"The Queen of Sheba will judge this generation and condemn it. She came from the ends of the earth to hear Solomon's wisdom, but you close your ears to someone far greater than Solomon. The men of Ninevah will judge this generation and condemn it because they repented when Jonah preached to them. Someone far greater than Jonah is here.

"No one lights a lamp and then puts it under a pail. No— everyone puts it on a stand so all can see when they come in. Your eye is the lamp of your body. When your eye is clear, your whole body fills with light, but when it is encrusted over, you are full of darkness. Be careful, then, that what you think is light in you is not actually darkness. When your whole body is full of light, it will all be lit up just like when a lamp gives you light all around."

Denouncing the Pharisees and Lawyers
(Luke 11: 37–54)

As I was speaking, a Pharisee came up and asked me to come for lunch, so I went to his house and reclined at the table. The Pharisee was disturbed when he saw that I didn't wash before lunch. Seeing the expression on his face, I said, "You Pharisees are always washing the outside of your cups and dishes, but inside yourselves you are full of greed and wickedness. You are foolish! Did not the maker of the outside make the inside as well? If you would make the inside clean by living to do good to others and to give to the needy, you wouldn't need to worry about the outside. It would naturally be taken care of.

"You Pharisees stand condemned, for you carefully tithe mint and rue and all the other herbs but show no concern for justice or the love of God. These are the things you should have done without overlooking the other. You Pharisees stand condemned, for you love the prominent seats in the synagogues and greetings reserved for the select few in the public square. Your condemnation is just. You are like unmarked graves that people unknowingly walk over, not seeing the corruption just below the surface."

One of the lawyers spoke up, "Teacher, when you say this, you condemn us as well."

I addressed the lawyers: "You lawyers stand condemned as well. You only overburden the people more by adding additional fine-tuning to the mountain of religious observances already in place—you never relax a single requirement.

"Condemnation on all of you! You decorate the tombs of the prophets killed by your fathers. So you testify to what your fathers did and approve of it, for they killed them and you build their tombs. God in his wisdom has said, 'I will send them prophets and apostles. They will kill some of them and some will be persecuted.' The blood of all the prophets murdered since the world began will be charged against this generation, from the blood of Abel to the blood of Zechariah, who was murdered between the altar and the sanctuary.[48] Yes, I assure you it will be charged against this generation. You lawyers stand condemned because you have buried the key to knowledge under your heap of tradition. You have refused to open the door yourselves and have discouraged others who try to enter."

As I left there, the scribes and Pharisees questioned me hard with all kinds of tricky questions, hoping to trap me into answers they could use against me to lead to my downfall.

Beware of Hypocrisy
(Luke 12:1–12)

The crowds had become so great that people trod on one another to get closer. I began teaching my disciples first. "At all costs, avoid creating a false image of yourself like the Pharisees. Hypocrisy is like yeast, which soon permeates all of your life. There is nothing covered up now that will not be uncovered; everything hidden will be brought out into the light. Whatever comment you have made in the dark, everyone will hear in the

---

[48] 2 Chronicles 24:21

light. Whatever delicious gossip you have whispered behind closed doors will be broadcast far and wide.

"This is my word to you, my friends: never fear those who can only kill your body and then have no more they can do. I can tell you who to fear. Fear the one who can not only kill your body, but afterward has the power to throw you into hell. Yes! That's the one to fear. You know that five sparrows are sold for two pennies, yet not one of them is overlooked by God. Did you know that God even knows the number of hairs on your head? Never fear; he values you far above many sparrows.

"Furthermore, let me tell you this: every person who owns me publicly before men the Son of Man will own before the angels of God in heaven. Every person who denies me before men I will deny before the angels of God. If anyone speaks a word against the Son of Man, they will be forgiven; but whoever speaks blasphemy against the Holy Spirit will never be forgiven.

"When they bring you before the leaders in synagogues or before rulers and authorities, don't worry about what answer you should give or what you should say. The Holy Spirit will give you the words to say even as you stand there."

Beware of Greed

(Luke 12:13–21, 32–34)

One of the crowd came up to me and asked, "Teacher, tell my brother to divide the inheritance with me."

But I replied, "What makes you think I am a judge or lawyer for you?" Having said that, I turned to the crowd. "Listen carefully! Whatever you do, be aware of what greed can do to you. Greed rates success in life by how much wealth you can collect. Let me assure you, the value of life has nothing to do with how much a person owns."

I went on to tell a parable: "A rich man's land produced abundant crops. So much so, he wondered how he was going to store everything. So he said to himself, 'What shall I do?' After thinking about it, he concluded, 'I have it! I'll take down my barns and build larger ones. Then I'll be able to store everything.

I can tell myself to take it easy, for I have enough for many years, so eat, drink and be happy.' But God said to him, 'You're a fool. This very night your life on earth will end. Then who will get all your wealth?' That's what happens to anyone who greedily hoards things for himself and doesn't consider what God would have him do."

Turning to my disciples, I said, "Don't you be afraid, my little flock, for the Father is pleased to give you the kingdom. Sell your possessions and give it all to the poor. Get yourselves purses that never grow old, filled with treasure in heaven where none of it will ever be lost. There no thief can go, nor can any moth ruin it, for where your treasure is, your heart will be there also."

The Faithful Servant
(Matthew 24:43–51, Luke 12:35–48)

I continued to teach my disciples, "As faithful servants, always be prepared. Have your robe in place with your sash on and your lamps lit. Be like men waiting for their master to arrive from the wedding feast, all ready to open the door when he comes and knocks. Happy are the servants who are alert and ready when the master comes. I assure you, he will have them sit at the table while he ties up his robe and serves them. Whether he comes before or after midnight, if he finds them ready and waiting, he will bless them. You know that if the owner of a house knew when a thief was coming, he would have been wide awake, preventing him from breaking in. You must always be ready too, because you have no way of knowing when the Son of Man will come."

Peter asked, "Lord, this parable—are you telling it just for us or is it for everyone?"

I replied, "Who do you think is the wise and faithful servant who is put in charge of the household by his master? He sees to it that everyone receives their food on time each meal. The master will bless that servant when he comes home and finds he

F. ARTHUR COOMBES

is faithfully doing everything right. I assure you, he will put him in charge of everything he owns.

"But if that servant says to himself, 'My master isn't coming for a long time,' and then proceeds to beat up the other servants and eat and get drunk, the master will arrive when he is not expected and he will cut him in pieces. The servant who knows what his master desires and then doesn't do it will be severely punished. The servant who did not know what his master expected of him will receive light punishment. Much will be expected of those who have been given much."

Some Effects of My Coming
(Luke 12:49–53)

Watching the crowds, I knew what my presence meant. My heart was heavy as I said to my disciples, "I have come and my coming will throw fire on the earth. How I wish it were already lit. I have a baptism of fire that I must be baptized with. What anguish of soul hangs over me until it is finished! Do you think I will bring peace on the earth? No! My presence brings division. From now on, in a house of five it will be three against two and two against three. Father will be against son and son against father. Mother will be against daughter and daughter against mother, mother-in-law against daughter-in-law and daughter-in-law against mother-in-law."

The Signs of the Times
(Luke 12:54–59)

I turned and spoke again to the crowds. "When you see a cloud coming from the west you say, 'Rain is coming,' and sure enough, it rains. When you feel the south wind blowing, you say, 'It's going to be a scorcher,' and sure enough, it happens. You hypocrites! You know how to read the signs of changing weather but you don't know how to understand the signs of the times.

"Why don't you judge for yourselves what is right? When your accuser goes with you to court, do everything you can along the way to settle the issue with him. You may get dragged to the judge and then handed over to the officer to be put in prison where you will never get out until you pay every penny."

Repent or Perish
(Luke 13:1–9)

There were some who had just arrived at that time who told about how Pilate had mixed the blood of some Galileans with their sacrifices. I replied to them, "Because they suffered this way, do you think these Galileans were worse sinners than any other Galileans? I assure you, no! Unless you repent, you will all eventually perish. What about the eighteen people who died in Jerusalem when the tower of Siloam fell? Do you think they were worse sinners than anyone else living in Jerusalem? Again I assure you, no! If you don't repent, you will all perish in the same way."

I went on to relate a parable: "A man had a fig tree in his vineyard. He looked for fruit on it but there wasn't any. So he said to his vinedresser, 'For three years I have looked for fruit on this fig tree and there has never been any. It's just wasting space, so cut it down.' The vinedresser replied, 'Sir, why not give it another chance? I'll dig around it and put some fertilizer on it. If there is no fruit next year, we'll cut it down.'"

A Crippled Woman Healed
(Luke 13:10–17)

One Sabbath I was teaching in one of the synagogues and a woman was there who had been oppressed by a spirit of infirmity for eighteen years. During all that time she was bent over, never able to stand up straight. My heart went out to her, so I called her over to me and laid hands on her, saying, "Woman, you are released from your oppression." Immediately she stood up straight and began joyfully praising God.

The ruler of the synagogue was indignant. "There are six days when people can work. If you want to be healed, come on those days, not on the Sabbath!"

I responded, "You hypocrites! Who doesn't untie his ox or his donkey from the manger on the Sabbath to lead it to water? Why, then, shouldn't this woman, a daughter of Abraham bound by Satan for eighteen years, be set free on the Sabbath day?" When I said this, all my opponents were shamed in front of the people. As for the people, they rejoiced at all the wonderful things they had seen me do.

The Seventy Return
(Matthew 11:25–30; Luke 10:17–24)

The seventy came back filled with joy, excitedly telling me, "Lord, even the demons are obedient to us in your name!"

I replied to them, "I saw Satan fall like a bolt of lightning from heaven. I tell you, I have given you the power to trample on snakes and scorpions and all the demonic powers, and nothing can ever hurt you. But don't allow this authority, incredible as it is, to be your greatest source of joy. The fact that the spirits are subject to you is nothing compared to the reality that your names are recorded in heaven forever."

The joy of the Holy Spirit poured over me, causing me to rejoice over these truths as I spoke to my Father: "I thank you, Father, Lord of heaven and earth, that you have concealed these facts from the brilliant scholars and men of insight and have revealed them instead to the childlike. Yes, Father, your gracious will was pleased to make it so."

I continued, "My Father has put everything under my authority. No one knows me, the Son, except my Father, and no one knows my Father except me and anyone else whom I choose to reveal him to. Come to me, everyone who is weary and struggling under heavy burdens, and I will give you rest. Get into harness with me and experience my ways, for I am meek and humble in heart and your soul will be at rest. Wearing my harness is effortless and sharing the burden together makes it light."

Speaking privately to my disciples, I said, "How blest your eyes are to see what you are now seeing. I assure you that many prophets and kings would have given anything to see what you are seeing and to hear what you hear. They did not live to see or hear anything like what you are experiencing right now."

At the Feast of Dedication
(John 10:22–39)

It was winter, and I was at the Feast of Dedication in Jerusalem.[49] I was walking in the portico of Solomon in the temple when a group of Jewish leaders surrounded me. They demanded, "How long are you going to keep us guessing? If you are the Christ, tell us the plain truth."

I responded, "I have told you but you don't believe. The miracles I do in my Father's name are proof of who I really am, but you still do not believe. The reason you disbelieve is because you are not my sheep. My sheep hear my voice; I know them and they follow me. They will never be lost because I give them eternal life. No one can ever take them from my embrace. They are a gift to me from my Father, the greatest of all. No one can grab them from my Father. My Father and I are one."

At this point the Jews picked up stones to throw at me, so I asked them, "For which of the many miracles my Father has empowered me to do are you stoning me?"

The Jews replied, "We aren't stoning you because of the miracles; we stone you for blaspheming because you make yourself equal with God even though you are obviously a man."

I said to them, "Isn't it written in your Law, 'I said you are gods?'[50] You know that Scripture cannot be changed. If those who receive the word of God are called gods, how can you say I am blaspheming when I say, 'I am the Son of God,' the one whom the Father set apart to be sent into the world? If I am not doing the things my Father does, then don't believe me. If I am doing the works of my Father, then believe the works I do, even if you cannot believe me. Then at least you can know that the

---

[49] The Feast of Dedication occurs in November–December.

[50] Psalm 82:6

Father is in me and I am in the Father." They tried to arrest me again but I slipped away from their control.

Leaving Jerusalem
(Luke 13:22–35; John 10:40–42)

After this, I left Jerusalem and went down to the other side of the Jordan to the place where John baptized in the beginning. I stayed there for some time and many came to me. They said, "John did not do miracles, but everything he said about this man is true." Many came to believe in me there.

I then traveled through various towns and villages, teaching as I went. I began working my way back toward Jerusalem. Someone came up to me and asked, "Lord, will there be few saved?"

So I said to them, "Do everything in your power to enter through the narrow door. I assure you, many will try to enter but they will not be able. When the master of the house has closed the door, many will stand outside and knock on the door. They will call out, 'Lord, open the door for us,' and he will reply, 'I don't know where you have come from.' They will go on, 'We dined with you; you taught us in our streets.' He will finally say, 'I told you, I don't know where you came from. Get away from here, all of you who do evil.' Many of you will cry out and grind your teeth in remorse when you see Abraham, Isaac and Jacob along with all the prophets in the kingdom of God while you are thrown out. People will come from everywhere—north, south, east and west—and feast in the kingdom of God. I tell you, many who are last will be first, and many who are first now will be last."

Right after I said this, some Pharisees came to tell me, "You better get out of here because Herod wants to kill you."

I replied to them, "Go and tell that fox, 'Look, I'm going to cast demons out and heal people today and tomorrow. I will finish up on the third day. No matter what you think, I will follow my course for these three days, for it's not possible for a prophet to be killed anywhere else but in Jerusalem.'"[51]

Having said that, my heart was heavy as I lamented, "Oh Jerusalem, Jerusalem, you have killed the prophets and stoned those who were sent to you. How often I have wanted to gather your children together under my care as a hen gathers her little chicks under her wings, but you wouldn't have anything to do with me. Look! Your house is desolate. I tell you, you will never see me again until you say, 'Blessed is he who comes in the Lord's name.'"

A Ruler's Invitation
(Luke 14:1–24)

One Sabbath a ruler, a Pharisee, invited me to eat at his home. There was a man right in front of me who had dropsy. They were all watching me intently, waiting to see what I would do. So I asked the lawyers and Pharisees, "Is it legal to heal on the Sabbath or not?" My question was met with stony silence. So I turned to the man and healed him. He went on his way. Addressing them all again, I said, "If one of you has a donkey or an ox that falls into a well on the Sabbath day, won't you immediately go and pull it out?" Again there was silence because they couldn't answer me.

I had been watching how the invited guests chose the places of honor at the table, so I said to them, "Whenever someone invites you to a marriage feast, don't sit in one of the prominent places. Suppose a special guest comes along with the host, who says to you, 'This place is reserved for this man. Please move down further.' Then, in front of all the guests, you are totally embarrassed as you take the lowest place. Instead, take the lowest place so that if the host comes along he may well say, 'Friend, move up to a higher place.' Then everyone will respect you. For those who are proud will be humiliated, and those who humble themselves will be honored."

---

[51] Luke 13:34–35; Matthew 23:37–39

I spoke to the host who had invited me. "When you provide a luncheon or a banquet, don't limit your invitations to your relatives or your wealthy associates. They are likely to invite you back and so you will be repaid. Rather, invite the street people, the lame and the blind, the single mothers and widows who cannot possibly repay you. You will be richly rewarded at the resurrection of the just."

One of those sitting at the table who heard this said, "Blest is the one who shall dine in the kingdom of God!"

Picking up on this, I related, "A man gave a great banquet one day. He had invited a large number of guests and, when the feast was prepared, he sent his servant to inform them that all was ready. But instead of coming they all began making excuses: 'I have purchased a field, so I need to go and see what it's like.' 'I just acquired five yoke of oxen, so I have to go and try them out,' and finally, 'I have just married a beautiful wife, so I can't come now.' The servant reported all this to the master. The master was angry, so he said to the servant, 'Quickly, go out into the streets and avenues of the city and bring in the poor, the homeless, the crippled and the blind.' The servant returned, 'Sir, I have done all that you asked and yet we still have room.' 'Okay then, go out beyond the city to the highways and byways and compel anyone you meet to come in so my house will be filled. I assure you, none of the invited guests will taste my banquet.'"

The Cost of Discipleship
(Luke 14:25–35)

At this time, great crowds were following me, so I confronted them: "If anyone seeks to follow me and does not put me first before his own father or mother or even before his own wife and children or his brothers and sisters, he cannot be my disciple. In fact, he has to put his own life on the line, pick up his cross and come follow me if he wants to be my disciple.

"If any of you wanted to build a tower, would you start right in without calculating the cost? You would sit down and do the math, wouldn't you? Otherwise, you might get the foundation done and then run out of money; you would be the laughing-stock of the whole town.

"Would a king, planning to confront another king, set out without seeking the advice of his generals first? He has to decide whether his 10,000 men are capable of defeating the other coming with 20,000. If his advisors say, 'No!' he will send an embassy while the other is still a long way away, seeking peace terms. I say, therefore, to you, whoever does not consider all that he has as rubbish cannot be my disciple. Salt is valuable, but if its taste has been washed out, it is useless. It's not even good for the land or the rubbish heap. Men simply throw it away. He who has ears to hear what I say, pay close attention."

The Lost Sheep
(Luke 15:1–7)

The tax collectors and sinners were all coming to me to hear what I was saying. Naturally, the scribes and Pharisees grumbled among themselves, saying, "This man not only welcomes sinners, he even goes so far as to eat with them."

So I told them all a parable: "If you had a hundred sheep and discovered one was missing, wouldn't you leave the 99 in the fold and go searching for the lost sheep until you found it? Then, when you found it, you would lay it on your shoulders and come home rejoicing to your friends and neighbors, saying, 'Celebrate with me; I have found my lost sheep!' In the same way, I assure you, there is more joy in heaven over one sinner repenting than over 99 righteous people who do not need to repent."

The Lost Coin
(Luke 15:8–10)

I related another parable. "Is there any woman who has ten silver coins who, if she finds out she has lost one, will not carefully search for it? She will light a lamp and sweep the house until she finds it. Then she will tell her friends and neighbors, calling on them to share her joy. In the same way, the angels of God rejoice over the repentance of one sinner."

The Lost Son
(Luke 15:11–32)

I continued on, "Once a man had two sons. The younger son came to his father one day, asking, 'Dad, I want my share of the inheritance now.' So the father divided all he had between his two sons.[52] It wasn't long before the younger son took off with his entire inheritance and moved to a distant country. There, he lived it up until he had wasted everything on wine, women and song. When he was down to his last penny, a famine swept across the land. He was destitute, so in desperation he took the only job he could find: feeding pigs in a farmer's field. He was so hungry he could have eaten the pods the pigs ate. No one offered him anything. He soon realized what a fool he had been. His mind went back to the pleasant life on his dad's farm, where the servants had all they could eat and more. Then he looked down at his rags and said to himself, 'Here I am, dying of starvation while my dad's servants are all well fed. I have only one option. I am going back to Dad. I will confess to him, "Father, I have sinned against God and against you. I no longer have any right to be called your son. I would be overjoyed just to be one of your servants."'

"So he got up on his feet and headed out on the long journey home. As he was approaching the old homestead, his dad saw him away off in the distance. It was the sight his tired old eyes had longed for. He leapt to his feet and took off down the road. Before his son could get a word out, the dad gave him a bone-crushing hug and kissed his weary face. When he found his tongue, he started his prepared speech, 'Father, I have sinned against God and against you. I don't have any right to be called your son.'

---

[52] Deuteronomy 21:17

"Before he could get the rest out, his dad was calling out to the servants, 'Quick! Bring the best robe and put it on him; put a ring on his finger and sandals on his feet. Kill the fatted calf and let's have a party! My son was dead but he's alive again; he was lost but is found.' Soon the house rocked with music, dancing and laughter.

"By now the older brother was coming in from the field. He heard the music and dancing, so he called over a servant to tell him what it was all about. The servant explained, 'Your brother has come home, so your father has killed the fatted calf because he has him back safe and sound.' Big brother stomped off toward the barn, his face red with anger, but his father came out to plead with him to come and celebrate. But he turned on his dad, 'I have served you all the years of my life, and have never disobeyed you in all that time. In all those years you never gave me a fatted calf to celebrate with my friends. Yet when this worthless son of yours comes home after he blew the entire inheritance you gave him on harlots, you kill the fatted calf for him!' With tears in his eyes, the father replied, 'Son, you are always here with me; everything you see here that is mine is also yours. It was suitable to celebrate because your brother was dead but now he is alive again, was lost but now he has been found.'"

The Crooked Business Manager
(Luke 16:1–18)

After this, I told a story to my disciples: "A rich man began to get reports that his business manager was cooking the books and things were going missing around the estate. So he called his manager up on the carpet. 'What's this I hear about you? Reports are getting back to me that your activities aren't all on the up and up. You're fired! But first I want you to prepare a complete audit of my affairs.'

"As the manager left the office, he said to himself, 'What am I going to do? With this blot on my record I'm not going to get hired anywhere else soon. I don't know a trade and I can't face sitting on the sidewalk downtown with a handful of pencils and my hat in front of me.' As he thought for a while, an idea came to him. 'My boss has quite a few men who owe him considerable amounts. I will do them all a favor and then they will feel indebted to me.' So he called the debtors in, one by one.

"The first arrived. 'How much do you owe us?' 'A hundred gallons of oil.' 'Here, take your promissory note and write me a new one for fifty.' This went on all day. A man who owed a hundred bushels of wheat left owing only eighty. And so it went.

"When the rich man got his audit, he realized what had happened. He couldn't help but admire the rascal's brilliant scheme. The children of the world's system are cleverer than the honest sons of light. Make use of what material assets you receive to benefit others. That way, if you run short, they will return the favor and your generous spirit will bring a reward in heaven. Honesty in small things reveals that you will be honest in handling large amounts. Dishonesty in small things proves that you can't be trusted in large things. If you can't even be trusted with the here-today-gone-tomorrow goods of this world, who's going to trust you with the true wealth from God? If you aren't trustworthy with what belongs to others, who will entrust you with what is yours? You cannot serve two masters. You will either hate the one and love the other, or you will devote yourself to the one and look down on the other. You cannot serve God and money at the same time."

Some Pharisees overheard me teaching this to my disciples. They were great lovers of money so they made a mockery of what I said. I turned to them, "You are the ones who go to great lengths to appear upright in men's eyes, but you don't fool God; he knows your hearts. The things that men put great stock in are detestable in the sight of God.

"The Law and the Prophets were all there was until John came. Now good news about the coming of the kingdom of God is being proclaimed and everyone is storming the gates. This does not mean the Law is now void. It would be easier for heaven and earth to pass away than for the smallest jot of the Law to be set aside. For instance, every man who divorces his wife to marry someone else commits adultery, and the man who marries a divorced woman commits adultery."

The Rich Man and Lazarus
(Luke 16:19–31)

I related a parable to warn about greed.

"There was a rich man who indulged himself to the limit. He dressed in gorgeous robes and feasted every day on the richest of foods and the best wines. At his gate lay a poor man named Lazarus, who was covered in sores which the dogs licked every day. Lazarus died and the angels carried him into the arms of Abraham. Eventually the rich man died and was buried in an ornate tomb after an elaborate funeral. The rich man went to hell where he was tormented. He looked up and saw Lazarus in Abraham's arms way off in the distance. So he called out, 'Father Abraham, take pity on me. Send Lazarus to dip his finger in water to cool my tongue, for I am constantly tortured by these flames.' But Abraham said, 'Son, don't forget that in your lifetime you indulged yourself with every luxury while Lazarus existed in wretchedness at your gate. Now he is comforted here while you are tormented. Besides this, there is an impassable canyon placed between us, so that no one can cross over in either direction.'

"Then the rich man said, 'I implore you to send Lazarus to my father's house because I have five brothers who need to be warned so they don't come into this terrible torment.' Abraham replied, 'They have Moses and the Prophets who they can listen to.' The rich man pleaded further, 'No, Father Abraham, they don't get it; but if someone rose from the dead they will repent.' But Abraham said, 'If they won't listen to Moses and the Prophets, they won't be convinced even if someone rises from the dead.'"

Teaching My Disciples
(Luke 17:3–10)

I said to my disciples, "Take care of one another; be your brother's keeper. If your brother sins, don't ignore it and go on your merry way. Help him to see where his error is. If he agrees with you and repents, then immediately forgive him. Even if he sins against you seven times in one day and turns to you each time, saying, 'I'm sorry, please forgive me,' you must forgive him seven times."

My disciples then said to me, "Increase our faith."

So I said to them, "If you had even as much faith as a mustard seed, you could command this mulberry tree, 'Be pulled up by the roots and get planted in the sea,' and it would obey."

I went on to speak about servanthood: "You know what is usual. If you have a servant plowing or looking after the sheep, when he comes in from the field, do you say, 'Come and sit down to eat'? No, you don't. You say to him, 'Make my supper for me and then serve me until I eat and drink my fill. After that, you can eat and drink.' Do you thank the servant for doing his normal job? Of course not. It's the same for you. When you have carried out all that you were ordered to do, you should say, 'We are not worthy servants. We have only done our regular duty.'"

Lazarus Raised
(John 11:1–46)

Lazarus was very sick. He lived in the village of Bethany with his sisters, Mary and Martha. This is the same Mary who anointed my feet with ointment and wiped them with her hair. The sisters sent word to me, "Lord, the one you love is very sick." When I received this, I said to my disciples, "This sickness is not fatal. God has allowed it to bring glory to him and also for the Son to be glorified through it." I greatly loved Martha, Mary and Lazarus, but I still needed to stay where I was for two more days.

After this, I said to my disciples, "Let's head back to Judea."

They replied, "Teacher, the last time we were there, you barely escaped being stoned. Now you want to go back there again?"

I explained, "You know there are twelve hours in the day. If you walk in the day, you don't stumble because there is plenty of light. If you walk in the night, you stumble because you don't have enough light. Our friend Lazarus has gone to sleep so I am going to wake him up."

My disciples spoke up, "Lord, if he is sleeping, he will get better."

I meant that he had died but they thought he was just peacefully resting, so I spoke plainly, "Lazarus is dead. For your sakes, I'm glad I wasn't there so you may believe. Come! Let's go to him."

Thomas, called the twin, said to the others, "Let's all go; we can all die with him."

When we arrived in Bethany, I was told Lazarus had already been dead four days. Bethany was only two miles east of Jerusalem, so many of the Jews came out to comfort Martha and Mary. When Martha heard I was approaching, she came out to meet me while Mary stayed in the house. She spoke with tears in her eyes, "Lord, if only you had been here, my brother would still be alive, yet I know that whatever you ask God for, he will give you."

I replied, "Your brother will rise again."

Martha responded, "I know he will rise on the last day at the resurrection."

I said to her, "I am the resurrection and the life. Everyone who lives and believes in me, even though their present life here will end, will live forever. Do you believe this?"

"Yes, Lord; I do believe you are the one expected to come into the world — the Christ, the Son of the living God." Having so said, she returned to the house, where she spoke to Mary privately so the others didn't hear, "The teacher is here; he is asking for you."

Mary quickly left the house and found me on the edge of town where Martha had met me. The Jews in the house thought

Mary had gone to weep at Lazarus' grave, so they followed her out. She fell at my feet as soon as she saw me, saying between her sobs, "Lord, if you had been here, my brother would not have died." When I saw her crying and the Jews also crying with her, I was shaken to the depths of my being. I managed to say to her, "Where is the grave?" Then my chest heaved as I broke into tears.

They said to me, "Lord, come and see." The Jews said to one another, "See how much he loved him!" Others murmured, "He opened the eyes of the blind; could he not keep this man from dying?"

Again, I was overcome with my emotions as we came to the tomb. It was a cave with a large stone rolled across the opening. I said, "Roll away the stone."

Martha spoke up, "Lord, by this time the odor will be terrible; he's been dead four days!"

I turned to her, "Martha, didn't I tell you that if you only believed, you would see the glory of God?" So with that, they rolled the stone away. Then I looked up to my Father and said, "Father, I thank you that you have heard me. I know you always hear me, but I have said this for the sake of those standing here that they may believe I was sent by you."

Then I cried out with a loud voice, "Lazarus, come out!" He came out, all wrapped in strips of fabric with a cloth over his face. "Unwrap him and let him go," I instructed.

Many of the Jews standing there believed in me when they saw what I did. But others went and reported to the Pharisees everything I had done.

The Jewish Council Meets
(John 11:47–54)

The chief priests and the Pharisees gathered the entire council together. They expressed their frustration. "What are we going to do? This man keeps doing many miracles. If we let him continue, the whole country will believe in him. Then the

Romans will come and wipe out our temple and the entire nation."

Caiaphas, the high priest that year, spoke to them all, "You don't understand at all. Don't you see it is better for us that one man die for the nation than have the whole nation destroyed?" This statement did not come from his own wisdom. As high priest that year he unknowingly prophesied that I would die for the nation. And not only for the nation, but for all the children of God scattered around the world, that they should be united as one body. From that day on, the council plotted how they might put me to death. As a result, I didn't go openly among the Jews. I withdrew for a time to a town called Ephraim near the wilderness, where my disciples and I stayed for a while.

The Ten Lepers
(Luke 17:11–19)

We then moved on to eastern Samaria near the border of Galilee. We entered a village where ten lepers met us. Standing at a distance, they called out to me, "Jesus, Master, have mercy on us."

I responded, "Go! Have the priests examine you." Even as they went, they were healed. One of them, a Samaritan, returned as soon as he saw he was healed. I heard him coming as he was loudly praising God all the way. He fell at my feet in gratitude, thanking me profusely. So I said, "Weren't there ten cleansed? What happened to the other nine? Did none of them come back to praise God except this Samaritan?"

Then I said to him, "Stand up! Go on your way. Your faith has brought you healing."

The Kingdom of God and My Return
(Luke 17:20–37)

On one occasion the Pharisees asked me when the kingdom of God was coming. I told them, "The kingdom of God is not coming with an observable, physical presence. You will never be able to say, 'It's over there!' or 'Here it is!' The kingdom of God is without boundaries. Understand this! The kingdom of God is already here right in the middle of you."

I went on from there, teaching my disciples, "There will be times coming when you would give anything to see even one of the days of the Son of Man, but you will not see it. There will be those who will claim, 'He's over here!' or 'There he is!' Don't pay any attention to them. Don't go to see if they are right. You will know the day when the Son of Man comes. Just as lighting flashes across the entire sky; that's how brilliant my return will be. But long before that happens, the Son of Man must endure great suffering. He will be rejected by the people of this age.

"When the Son of Man returns, it will be just like the days of Noah. They ate and drank; they got married and gave their daughters in marriage right up until the day Noah entered the ark. The flood came and destroyed them all. It was the same when Lot lived in Sodom. They ate, drank, bought, sold, planted and built. But the day Lot walked out of Sodom, fire and brimstone poured down and they were all destroyed. That's how it will be when the Son of Man reveals himself. On that day, if one is on his roof, he must not come down to gather his things in the house to take them away. If one is in the field, he must not go back to the house. Remember what happened to Lot's wife. Whoever tries to cling to his life will lose it, but whoever loses his life will save it. I assure you, on that night two men will be sleeping in one bed; one will be taken, the other will be left. Two women will be grinding flour together; one will be taken, the other will be left."

My disciples asked, "Lord, where will this happen?"

I replied, "Wherever the body is, the vultures will gather."

About Prayer

(Luke 18:1–14)

I told them a parable to teach them to never get discouraged about praying. "There was a city where a judge presided who had no respect for people or even for God. In the same city lived a widow, who kept coming to the judge, asking, 'Provide justice for me against my opponent.' For some time he turned her down, but eventually he said to himself, 'This widow is wearing me out. I couldn't care less about her and I don't care what God thinks, but to get her off my back, I'll see she gets justice.'"

I then nailed the point down: "Listen to what the godless judge said. Don't you think God will justify his children who petition him day and night? I assure you he will, and he will do it speedily. Yet in spite of that, when the Son of Man returns, will he find faith on the earth?"

Then I related this parable for the self-righteous who looked down on everybody else. "Two men went into the temple to pray. One of them was a Pharisee, and the other, a tax collector. The Pharisee boldly stood up close, 'God, I thank you that I'm not like other men—thieves, swindlers, immoral—or even like that tax collector. I fast twice every week and I tithe everything I get.' The tax collector, on the other hand, stayed in the outer court. He didn't even look up; he thumped his breast in remorse, saying, 'God, have mercy on me, a sinner!' I assure you, this man went home forgiven more than the other. For everyone who praises himself will be humiliated, and everyone who humbles himself will be lifted up."

About Marriage and Divorce
(Matthew 19:1–12; Mark 10:1–12)

I crossed the Jordan into Perea. Large crowds began to gather again so I healed many and taught them. Some Pharisees came up to me to test me. They asked, "Is it legal for a man to divorce his wife for any cause?"

I replied, "Haven't you read that God who made them in the beginning made them male and female?[53] He said, 'For this reason, a man shall leave his father and mother and be joined to his wife and the two shall become one flesh.'[54] So they aren't two but one. Therefore, what God has joined together, let no man separate."

---

[53] Genesis 1:27; 5:2
[54] Genesis 2:24

The Pharisees broke in, "Why, then, did Moses allow a man to give his wife a writ of divorce and put her away?"

I told them, "Moses allowed this because of your hard hearts, but from the beginning it wasn't this way."

When we went into the house, my disciples brought this subject up again. So I said to them, "Whoever divorces his wife and marries another commits adultery, unless the divorce is because of adultery. And if a woman divorces her husband and marries another, she commits adultery."

My disciples commented, "If this is how it is between a man and his wife, it isn't wise to get married." I replied, "Not all men can live up to this concept—only those who are given the ability. There are men who are eunuchs from birth. Others have been made eunuchs by men. Still others have made themselves eunuchs for the sake of the kingdom of God. For those who are able to receive this, let them receive it."

Blessing the Children
(Matthew 19:13–15; Mark 10:13–16; Luke 18:15–17)

They were bringing the children for me to lay hands on them and pray. My disciples started to reprove them, but when I saw what they were doing, I was very displeased. So I said to them, "Allow the children to come to me; don't prevent them, for the kingdom of God belongs to ones like these. I tell you the truth: only those who receive the kingdom of God like a child will ever enter it." Then I took the children in my arms, blessing them and laying my hands on them.

The Rich Young Ruler
(Matthew 19:16–30; Mark 10:17–31; Luke 18:18–30)

As we started out to travel further, a young ruler ran up and knelt in front of me. "Good teacher, what good deed can I do to gain eternal life?"

I answered, "Why do you call me good? No one is good except God. If you want to live on, keep the commandments."

He replied, "Which ones?"

So I said, "You shall not kill, you shall not commit adultery, you shall not steal, you shall not lie, honor your father and mother and love your neighbor as you do yourself."

The young man responded, "Teacher, I have kept all these from my youth. What do I still need to do?"

I could not help but love this young man, so I said to him, "You lack only one thing. Sell everything you have; give it to the poor and you will have treasure in heaven. Then come and follow me."

When he heard this, the anticipation in his eyes faded and great sadness took its place. He rose to his feet and sorrowfully turned away with a downcast look, for he was very rich. With tears in my eyes, I watched him go. Then I turned to my disciples, "It is very hard for the rich to enter the kingdom of God." My disciples were astonished at what I had said, so I repeated, "Children, it is very hard to enter the kingdom of God! A camel can go through the eye of a needle more easily than a rich man can enter the kingdom of God."

My disciples were amazed even more at that statement so they said, "Who, then, can be saved?"

As I scanned their puzzled faces, I replied, "For men, it is impossible, but not for God. All things are possible with God."

Peter spoke up, "We have left everything to follow you. What shall we have?"

My heart went out to them as I assured them, "I tell you the truth, in the new age, when the Son of Man sits on his glorious throne, you who have left everything to follow me will also sit on twelve thrones. You will judge the twelve tribes of Israel. Anyone who has left houses or wife or brothers or sisters or parents or children or lands for my sake and for the gospel will receive one hundred times more now in this age, and in the coming age, eternal life. Many that are first now will be last and many that are last now will be first."

Parable of the Vineyard Workers
(Matthew 20:1–16)

"The kingdom of God is like a landowner who went out early in the day to hire workers for his vineyard. The workers agreed to work for a dollar a day, so he sent them into the vineyard. Around nine o'clock he found others standing around in the marketplace, so he sent them into his vineyard, assuring them they would be paid appropriately. Later, he went out at noon and at three, doing the same thing. Finally, at five he still found people standing around the marketplace. 'Why are you standing here all day?' he asked. 'Because no one has hired us.' So he sent them into his vineyard too.

"At the end of the day, he said to his manager, 'Call in the workers and pay them, beginning with the last ones hired.' Those who came at five all received a dollar like the others. Those who came first saw this so they expected more. They complained to the landowner, 'These guys only worked an hour, yet you paid them the same as us. We worked through the heat of the entire day.' The landowner responded, 'Comrades, what have I done wrong? Didn't I pay you what you agreed to work for? Take your dollar and go. Am I not allowed to be generous with my money; after all, it is mine to use, isn't it?' So the last are first and the first, last."

Telling My Disciples About My Death
(Matthew 20:17–19; Mark 10:32–34; Luke 18:31–34)

We were on the road going toward Jerusalem. As I marched along ahead of them, some were amazed while others were afraid. It was time to take the twelve aside to tell them what was going to happen to me. "You are aware by now that we are going up to Jerusalem. Everything the prophets wrote about the Son of Man is going to be fulfilled. I am going to be arrested by the chief priests and the scribes; they will condemn me to death and I will be handed over to the secular authorities. They will make fun of me, treat me barbarically and spit on me. Finally, they will kill me—but on the third day I will rise again." My disciples didn't grasp anything I was saying, for it was hidden from them.

The Request of James and John
(Matthew 20:20–28; Mark 10:35–45)

One day James and John came to me with their mother. She knelt before me, asking, "Will you do for my sons what they request?"

Looking at them, I said, "What do you want?"

They replied, "When you come into your glory, command that one of us may sit on your right hand and the other on the left."

I said, "You have no idea what you are asking. Can you drink the cup I will soon drink or endure the baptism I will be baptized with?"

"Yes, we are able."

"Then you will drink the cup I will drink and experience the baptism I will be baptized with. As for sitting on my right and left hand, I do not even decide who that will be. That position is set aside for whoever it has been assigned by my Father."

When the other ten heard this, they were angry with James and John. So I called them all together to tell them, "You know how the leaders of the nations lord it over everyone and the wealthy assert their authority. That is not how it will be among you. Whoever strives to be great must serve everyone. If you want to be first, then you must become the slave of all the others. Even I, the Son of Man, did not come to be served. Rather, I came to serve and to give my life to pay the ransom for many."

Zacchaeus
(Luke 19:1–10)

As I entered Jericho, large crowds surrounded me. There was a rich man named Zaccheus in the town; he was the chief tax collector. He wanted to see me, but because he was short, he could not see over the crowd. So he ran ahead of me and climbed a sycamore tree. When I came to the tree, I looked up and said to him, "Zacchaeus, climb right down; I'm coming to your house today." He climbed down immediately and joyfully accompanied me to his house.

Some in the crowd murmured, "Doesn't he know what a sinner that man is—and he's going to eat with him?"

After dining, Zaccheus stood up and said, "Lord, I give half of my goods to the poor, and if I have cheated anyone, I replace whatever I took with four times as much."

I said to everyone, "Today salvation has come to this home, for he is also a son of Abraham. The Son of Man came to seek and to save people that were lost."

Blind Bartimaeus
(Matthew 20:29–34; Mark 10:46–52; Luke 18:35–43)

Taking leave of Zaccheus, we headed out of the city on our way to Jerusalem. As we went out of the gate, a large crowd accompanied us. A blind beggar named Bartimaeus, the son of Timaeus, was sitting by the roadside along with another blind man. When they heard that I was coming, they started shouting, "Jesus! Son of David, take pity on us." Many in the crowd, annoyed by their loud cries, kept telling them to cool it. But they only shouted louder, "Jesus! Son of David, take pity on us."

When I got near enough to hear them, I said to those nearby, "Call them over." So they called out to Bartimaeus and his friend.

They encouraged the blind men, "Your cries have been heard. Jesus is calling you."

So they stood up and were brought to me. I asked them, "What is it you want me to do for you?"

They pleaded, "Lord, open our eyes so we can see."

As I looked at them, I was moved with compassion. So I touched their eyes—immediately they were able to see perfectly. I told them, "Your faith has healed you." Their joy knew no limits as they followed me along the road. Their pitiful cries were now replaced with joyful cries of glory to God. When the people saw this, they joined with them, praising God along the way.

The Nobleman's Return
(Luke 19:11–28)

As we continued up the road to Jerusalem, wildly different emotions surged through the throng. I knew my time was imminent. My disciples experienced fear and foreboding. At the same time, the idea that a glorious revealing of the kingdom of God was about to happen filled some people's minds with expectancy and excitement. To counteract this false expectation, I told them a parable.

"A nobleman was about to leave for a far country, where he was going to be crowned king. As he would be gone some time, he called together ten of his servants. He gave each of them 1,000 dollars, saying to them, 'Do business with this money until I return. See what you can earn.' Meanwhile, his citizens hated him so much they sent a delegation after him, stating, 'We will not have this man rule over us.'

"After his coronation, he returned and called the ten servants together to see how they did with the money entrusted to them. One of them spoke up, 'Lord, I have gained 10,000 dollars more with your money.' He said to him, 'Very well done, my good servant! Because you have been faithful with this small amount, you will administer ten cities.' A second one shared, 'Lord, I have been able to make five thousand with your money.' To him, he said, 'Good, you will administer five cities.' Finally, another servant came forward, carrying the original thousand dollars that he had hidden in a cloth bag. He held it out, saying, 'Lord, here is your money, safe and sound. I didn't dare risk trading it because I feared what you would do. I know you are a harsh man, demanding what you never give out and expecting a harvest where you haven't even planted.' The master said to him, 'You have condemned yourself by what you just said. So I'm a harsh man who demands what I never gave out, am I? And I expect to harvest what I haven't planted? At least you could have deposited my money in the bank so it gained interest.' So he said to the other servants looking on, 'Take the money from this man and give it to the one who earned 10,000 dollars.' The servants objected, 'But Lord, he already has ten thousand.' 'I tell you, to everyone who has, more will be given, and to those who have little, even what they have will be taken from them. As for these rebels who don't want me to be their ruler, bring them here and put them to death.'"

Having said this, I pressed on ahead along the road up to Jerusalem.

At Bethany
(Matthew 26:6–13; Mark 14:3–9; John 11:55–57; 12:1–11)

As we approached Jerusalem, the crowds were already there, going through the purification in readiness to celebrate the Passover.[55] They were looking for me, so they said to one another, "Do you think he will come to the feast?" Already, the chief priests and the Pharisees had issued orders that if anyone saw me they were to let them know so they could arrest me.

Six days before the Passover, I arrived at Bethany. I went to the house of Simon the leper. Lazarus was there, whom I had raised from the dead, and Martha served us all supper. Mary came in with an alabaster jar of very expensive perfume; it was a pound of pure nard. She broke the jar and poured the nard on my head. She also used some of it to anoint my feet, drying them with her hair. The beautiful fragrance completely filled the whole house.

Judas Iscariot, the one who would betray me, spoke out in indignation, "What a waste! Why, this ointment could have fetched a year's wages and been given to the poor." He didn't say this because he cared for the poor. The poor were the least of his concern; he kept the money bag and often stole what was put in it.

I responded in no uncertain terms, "How dare you criticize this woman. Leave her alone! She has done a beautiful thing to me. You will always have the poor with you, but you will not always have me. You can give to the poor at any time—as you

---

[55] See Numbers 19:9–10.

should. She has done the only thing she could; she has anointed my body for burial beforehand. I assure you, what Mary has done will be told everywhere the gospel is preached throughout the whole world in remembrance of her."

When the crowds got word that I had arrived in Bethany, many of them came out of Jerusalem to see me. They also came to see Lazarus, whom I had raised from the dead. The chief priests were even planning to put Lazarus to death because many Jews came to believe in me because of him.

The Triumphal Entry
(Matthew 21:1–11; Mark 11:1–11; Luke 19:29–44; John 12:12–19)

The next day, I took my disciples and left Bethany to go to Jerusalem. As we approached the Mount of Olives, I said to two of my disciples, "Go into the village in front of us. Just as you enter it, you will see a donkey and her colt tied there. The colt has never been ridden. Untie it and bring it to me. If anyone asks why you are untying it, tell them, 'The Lord needs it; he will return it shortly.'" This fulfilled what was prophesied about me: "Rejoice daughter of Zion! Look! Your king is coming to you, humble and riding on a donkey's colt."[56]

My disciples found the colt just as I said, right there in the street, tied by a door. The owners asked, "What are you doing, untying that colt?"

They answered, "The Lord needs it." So the owners let it go and my disciples returned with the colt. They threw their cloaks on it for me to sit on.

The crowd who had come to the feast heard I was coming into the city, so they took palm branches and came out to meet me. They called out, "Hosanna! Blessed is he who comes in the name of the Lord. Blessings on the King of Israel." Many people spread their clothes on the road while others spread branches cut from the fields. The crowd from Bethany, who had seen Lazarus raised from the tomb, had shared the news of this

---

[56] Zechariah 9:9

miracle far and wide. It was on account of this that many came out. As we approached the descent from the Mount of Olives, the entire crowd both in front of and behind me burst out in even louder rejoicing, "Blessed be the king who comes in the name of the Lord. Peace in heaven and glory in the highest."

The Pharisees were incensed, "Teacher, listen to what they say! Stop your disciples!"

I replied, "I assure you, if they were silenced, the very stones would cry out!"

Then the Pharisees said to one another, "There is nothing we can do. Look how the whole world has gone after him."

As I looked out over the city below, my emotions overwhelmed me. I burst into tears, saying, "If only you knew today the conditions that would have brought you peace! But now it is too late; they are hidden from your eyes. The days are coming when your enemies will build earthworks against your walls; they will completely surround you, leaving no escape. You will be leveled to the ground with you and your children destined for destruction. Not one stone will be left upon another because you did not know the day you were visited."

When I entered the city, the entire place was alarmed. People were asking, "Who is this?"

The crowds that flowed in with me said, "This is Jesus, the prophet from Nazareth in Galilee." I went into the temple, and after looking around at everything, I headed back out to Bethany with my disciples because it was already late.

The Fig Tree
(Matthew 21:18–19; Mark 11:12–14)

As I was going into the city in the morning, I was hungry. I saw a fig tree in the distance, so when we came to it I looked for fruit on it, but there was nothing but leaves. It wasn't the season for figs. I said to it, "May no one ever eat fruit from you again." My disciples overheard what I said.

Cleansing the Temple
(Matthew 21:12–17; Mark 11:15–19; Luke 19:45–48)

We came to Jerusalem and I entered the temple. Conditions had returned to the way they were early in my ministry. So I drove out the merchants selling livestock and pigeons and overturned the money-changer tables just as I did before. I wouldn't even allow anyone to carry anything through the temple. Speaking to those standing there, I said, "It is written, 'My house shall be called a house of prayer for all nations.'[57] You have made it into a den of robbers." The chief priests and the scribes overheard me.

Then the lame and the blind came to me in the temple, and I healed all who came. The chief priests and the scribes saw all the miracles, but they only complained because they heard the children calling out in the temple, "Hosanna to the Son of David."

They said to me, "Do you hear what these children are saying?"

I answered, "Yes, and haven't you read, 'Out of the mouths of little children and infants you have perfected praise'?"[58]

The chief priests, scribes and leaders of the people tried to find a way to kill me, but they couldn't find a way to do it because the crowds listened to my every word. My teaching amazed them. As evening came, I returned to Bethany for the night.

The Fig Tree Withered
(Matthew 21:20–22; Mark 11:20–26)

As we walked past the fig tree in the morning, my disciples were astounded to see it completely withered right down to its roots. Peter said to me, "Master, look at the fig tree you cursed. How could it dry up so fast?"

---

[57] Isaiah 56:7

[58] Psalm 8:2

I said to them, "If you have faith in God, I assure you, you will be able to do things far greater than what has happened to this fig tree. You will be able to say to this mountain, 'Rise up and be thrown into the sea.' If you don't doubt in your heart, but believe, what you say will happen. Whatever you ask for in prayer—believing—you will receive your request. Whenever you are praying, always forgive anyone who has harmed you, for then your Father in heaven can forgive any harm you have done to others."

My Authority Challenged
(Matthew 21:23–27; Mark 11:27–33; Luke 20:1–8)

When we entered the temple, the chief priests, scribes and elders came up to me while I was teaching. They asked, "Where do you get the authority to do these things? Who did you get it from?"

I replied, "I have a question to ask you. If you answer my question, I will answer yours. Tell me, was the baptism of John from heaven or from men?"

I waited while they debated between themselves. "If we say 'from heaven,' he will say, 'Why didn't you believe him, then?' But if we say, 'From men,' this large crowd will stone us, for they are all convinced John was a real prophet."

So they came back to me, "We don't know."

I responded, "Neither am I going to tell you under what authority I do these things."

Parable of the Two Sons
(Matthew 21:28–32)

I began to teach in parables. I said, "Tell me what you think. A man had two sons. He told the first, 'Son, I want you to work in the vineyard today.' The son answered, 'I'm not going to.' Afterward he felt guilty, so he went and worked. The man then went to his second son and told him the same thing. The second son said, 'Yes, I will go,' but afterward he didn't go. Which of the two carried out his father's will?"

They answered, "The first."

Then I said to them, "The tax collectors and harlots go into the kingdom of God before you. For John came proclaiming the way of righteousness and you didn't believe him, but the tax collectors and harlots believed him. Even after you saw their repentance, you still didn't turn and believe him."

Parable of the Evil Husbandmen
(Matthew 21:33–46; Mark 12:1–12; Luke 20:9–19)

"A man planted a vineyard. He planted a hedge around it, dug a pit for the winepress and built a tower. He rented it to tenant farmers and left for another country. When it was time to harvest the grapes, however, he sent a servant to gather his share of the crop. The tenants beat up the servant and sent him away with nothing. He continued to send servants, but they were all shamefully treated. Some were beaten or wounded while still others were even stoned and killed. The owner was at his wit's end so he said to himself, 'What shall I do? I know! I will send my dearly loved son. They should at least respect him.' But as soon as the tenants saw him, they said to one another, 'Here comes the heir. If we kill him, the estate will become ours.' So they killed him and threw his body out beyond the vineyard. What will the owner of the vineyard do when he comes?"

They replied, "He will kill those tenants and find others." Some listening said, "God forbid that such a thing could happen."

I continued "Haven't you read what the Scriptures say? 'The stone that was thrown away by the builders has become the chief cornerstone. This is what the Lord has done; we look on with astonishment.'[59] Whoever falls on that stone will be shattered and anyone that stone falls on will be pulverized. I can assure you of this: the kingdom of God will be taken away from this nation; it will be given to a people who will produce the fruit of the kingdom."

---

[59] Psalm 118:22–23

When the chief priests and Pharisees heard my parables, they recognized that I was speaking about them. They attempted to arrest me right then and there, but they were afraid of the crowds, so they just went away.

Parable of the King's Son's Wedding
(Matthew 22:1–14)

I related another parable. "The kingdom of God can be likened to a king who prepared a marriage feast for his son. When all was ready, he sent his servants to call the invited guests, but they wouldn't come. So he sent out more servants, telling them, 'Go out and urge them to come. Tell them, "The dinner is ready, oxen and fatted calves are dressed. Come to the marriage feast."' Most of those invited laughed it off. They went off to their farms, some to their businesses. Others beat up the servants and killed them. The king was furious. He sent his army to kill the murderers and burn their city. He then said to his servants, 'The wedding is ready, but the invited guests weren't worthy. Go out to the streets and invite as many as you can find.' The servants did as they were told. They brought in good and bad until the hall was filled. When the king came to see the guests, he saw a man who hadn't put on a wedding garment, so he asked him, 'Friend, how did you come in without a wedding garment?' The man was speechless. The king ordered the attendants, 'Tie this man up, hand and foot, and throw him into outer darkness where men will cry out and gnash their teeth.' Many are called but few are chosen."

Taxes to Caesar
(Matthew 22:15–22; Mark 12:13–17; Luke 20:20–26)

The Pharisees got together to find a way to get me in trouble with the Roman authorities. They sent out people to listen to everything I said to see if they could trap me. They finally decided to send a delegation of Pharisees and Herodians. Pretending sincerity, they came with their prepared speech: "Teacher, we know that you teach the truth without regard for any man's opinion, for you only teach the message of God. We would like to know what you think about paying taxes to Caesar. Is it legal for us Jews to pay taxes to Caesar or not?"

Easily recognizing their intent, I answered, "You hypocrites, why do you try to trap me? Bring me a coin." So they handed me a coin. "Whose image and inscription is this?" I asked.

"Caesar's," they replied.

"Then pay to Caesar what belongs to Caesar, and to God what belongs to God." They went away amazed at my answer, having nothing more they could say.

The Sadducees' Question
(Matthew 22:23–33; Mark 12:18–27; Luke 20:27–40)

That same day, the Sadducees came with a question. They did not believe there was any resurrection, so they proposed this scenario: "Teacher, Moses wrote that if a man dies, leaving a wife but no children, then his brother must marry his widow to raise up children for the dead brother.[60] Now there were seven brothers. The first one married but died before they had any children. So the second brother married the widow, but he died without leaving any children for his brother. The same thing happened to all seven. Finally, the widow died. In the resurrection, whose wife will she be?"

I replied, "This shows why you are wrong because you don't know the Scriptures or the power of God. People in this age marry, but those who are worthy to enter the coming age will not marry, for they will live forever. They will be like the angels in heaven, being children of God.

"As for the resurrection from the dead, even Moses spoke about it in the account of the burning bush. When God spoke to him, he said, 'I am the God of Abraham and the God of Isaac and the God of Jacob.'[61] He is not the God of the dead but of the living, for all come to live in him. You are quite wrong."

---

[60] Deuteronomy 25:5–6

[61] Exodus 3:15

The crowd was astonished at my answer. Some of the scribes who were there said, "Teacher, your answer is very good." After that, no one dared try to trap me again.

The Lawyer's Question
(Matthew 22:34–40; Mark 12:28–34)

One of the scribes, a lawyer, came up as I was answering the Sadducees' question. He saw that I answered well so he asked, "Which is the greatest commandment of all?"

I replied, "The greatest is this: 'Hear, O Israel! The Lord our God, the Lord is one, and you shall love the Lord your God with all your heart, and with all your soul, and with all your mind, and with all your strength.'[62] The second is like it: 'You shall love your neighbor as yourself.'[63] The entire Law and the Prophets depend on these two commandments."

The scribe responded, "Teacher, you have spoken the truth! There is but one God; no other exists. To love him with all our heart, with all our understanding, with all our soul, with all our strength, and to love our neighbors as ourselves is more important than all the burnt offerings and sacrifices the Law requires."

I saw how wisely he answered, so I said, "You are not far from the kingdom of God." No one asked any more questions.

About David and the Messiah
(Matthew 22:41–46; Mark 12:35–37; Luke 20:41–44)

A group of Pharisees were gathered together as I taught in the temple, so I decided to ask them a question: "What do you think about the Christ—whose son is he?"

They answered, "The Son of David."

"How do you explain, then, that David, speaking by the Holy Spirit, called him Lord when he said, 'The Lord said to my Lord, "Sit at my right side until I put your enemies under your

---

[62] Deuteronomy 6:4–5
[63] Leviticus 19:18

feet"'?[64] If David himself calls him Lord, in what sense is he his son?" No one was able to give me a word of an answer. The large crowd gladly listened to me.

Warning About Jewish Leaders
(Matthew 23:1–12; Mark 12:38–40; Luke 20:45–47)

I told the crowd and my disciples, "The scribes and Pharisees officially explain the Law to you, so carry out whatever they tell you, but don't do what they do. They preach, but they don't practice what they preach. They do everything for show so that people will see them; they carry extra large Scripture boxes[65] and put long tassels on their long robes.[66] They love the nods of recognition in the marketplace, the front seats in the synagogues and the most honored positions at banquets. They love to be known as teachers. They use legal tricks to rob widows of their homes and then make a show by praying long prayers. Their greater condemnation will be justified.

"Do not allow people to call you 'teacher,' for you have only one teacher; you are all brethren. Don't call any man on earth 'father,' for you have only one Father and he is in heaven. Neither should any of you be called 'master,' for you have only one master, the Christ. The greatest among you will be your servant. Those who exalt themselves will be humiliated, but those who walk in humility will be exalted."

Warning the Scribes and Pharisees
(Matthew 23:13–36)

"Misery awaits you, scribes and Pharisees, hypocrites! You put the kingdom of God out of reach of anyone else. You refuse to enter it yourselves and you make sure no one else does who wants to.

---

[64] Psalm 110:1
[65] See Deuteronomy 6:8.
[66] Numbers 15:37–40

"Misery awaits you, scribes and Pharisees, hypocrites! You search the world to make one single convert. Once you have him, you make him twice the child of hell that you are.

"Misery awaits you, blind guides. You say, 'If anyone swears by the temple, what he says means nothing; it isn't binding. But if anyone swears by the gold on the temple it is binding; he must fulfill his promise.' You blind fools! Which is greater, the gold or the temple which makes the gold sacred? You also say, 'If anyone swears by the altar, what he says means nothing; it isn't binding. But if anyone swears by the gift on the altar it is binding; he must fulfill his promise.' You are blind! Which is greater, the gift on the altar or the altar that makes the gift sacred? Therefore, whoever swears by the altar swears by it and everything on it. Whoever swears by the temple swears by it and by God who lives in it. He who swears by heaven swears by the throne of God and by God who sits on it.

"Misery awaits you, scribes and Pharisees, hypocrites! You carefully tithe mint, dill and cumin, but you ignore the important commands in the Law: justice, mercy and faith. These are the things you should have majored in while not neglecting the others. You are blind guides—you strain out the gnat and then swallow a camel!

"Misery awaits you, scribes and Pharisees, hypocrites! You polish up the outside of the cup and plate but the inside is full of dirt, unchecked greed and self-indulgence. You blind Pharisees! Clean the inside first; then the outside will also be clean.

"Misery awaits you, scribes and Pharisees, hypocrites! You are like tombs painted white—lovely on the outside but full of rotting bones and filth on the inside. You look so righteous when people see you, but inside you are just the opposite: full of hypocrisy and sinful lusts.

"Misery awaits you, scribes and Pharisees, hypocrites! You build beautiful tombs for the prophets and decorate the monuments honoring the righteous. You say, 'If we had been alive in the times of our fathers, we would never have helped kill the prophets.' By saying this, you testify to the truth that you are the sons of those who murdered the prophets. Fill up, then, the cup of sin your fathers began. You snakes, you nest of poison, how do you hope to escape the damnation of hell? I will send you prophets, wise men and scribes; some you will kill or crucify. Others you will beat up in your synagogues and pursue from town to town. Upon you will come the condemnation for all the righteous blood shed on the earth—from the innocent blood of Abel to the blood of Zechariah, the son of Barachiah, whom you murdered between the temple and the altar. I assure you, all this will fall on this generation."

The Widow's Gift
(Mark 12:41–44; Luke 21:1–4)

One day, I sat down opposite the collection box, where I watched the crowds donating money. Many rich people put in large amounts. Then I saw a poor widow come and drop in two small copper coins worth about a penny. I called my disciples over, drawing their attention to the widow. "I want you to notice this poor widow. She has put in more than anyone else contributing to the collection box. Everyone else put something in from their abundance, but she, from her extreme poverty, has put in everything she has, her entire living."

The Greeks Seek Me
(John 12:20–43)

Among those worshipping at the feast were some Greeks. Some of them came to Philip, who came from Bethsaida in Galilee. They said to him, "We want to see Jesus." Philip told Andrew, so together, they came and told me.

Their request brought sharply to mind my purpose for coming, so I replied to Philip and Andrew, "The time has come for me to be glorified. This is the truth: unless a grain of wheat drops into the soil and dies, it remains by itself, but if it dies, it produces many grains. Whoever loves their life loses it, but whoever rejects their life in this world will keep it for eternity. For anyone to serve me, he must follow me; wherever I am, my servant will be there with me. Anyone who serves me will be honored by my Father.

"Now my soul is deeply stirred! What can I say?" I paused. Barely able to contain my emotions, I looked up, "Father, can you save me from this hour?" The words were no sooner out of my mouth than I knew what the answer had to be. I shouted, "No! For this very hour, I came! Father, glorify your name!"

Then I heard my Father's voice, "I have glorified it, and I will do it again!"

The crowd standing there heard his voice. Many of them said it thundered. Others said, "An angel spoke to him."

I said to them, "My Father's voice came to convince you, not me. Now! The world is being judged. Now! The ruler of this world will be thrown out. Now! I will be lifted up from the earth and all men will be drawn to me."

Saying this, I indicated by what kind of death I would die. This mystified the crowd, "We have understood from the Law that the Christ lives forever. Why do you say the Son of Man must be lifted up? Who, then, is this Son of Man?"

I replied, "Now the light is with you for only a very little while. Walk with the light while you have it so the darkness does not overwhelm you. Those overwhelmed by the darkness do not know where they are going. You must believe in the light while the light is here. If you do that, you can become sons of the light." When I finished saying this, I hid myself from them and quickly left.

Though I had done many miracles in the sight of everyone, they still couldn't believe in me. It was the fulfillment of what Isaiah the prophet said: "Lord, who has believed our testimony? Who will receive the revelation of his power to save?"[67] Because of this, they could not believe. When Isaiah saw my glory, I told him, "I have blinded their eyes and hardened their hearts so their eyes can't see or their hearts understand. They cannot turn to me to be healed."[68] In spite of this, even many of the

---

[67] Isaiah 53:1
[68] Isaiah 6:10

authorities believed in me, but they didn't publicly admit it because they feared the Pharisees. They didn't want to be thrown out of the synagogue; the praise of men was more important to them than the praise of God.

My Summary
(John 12:44–50)

I cried out to the crowds, "Whoever believes in me doesn't only believe in me but in the one who sent me! Whoever sees me sees the one who sent me! My coming sheds a bright light in a dark world. The one who believes in me will never be left in the darkness. I am not going to judge anyone who hears my words and does not obey them because I did not come to judge the world—I came to save the world. Anyone who rejects me and my words already has a judge; the words they heard me speak will be their judge on the last day. That's because my Father who sent me told me what to say and to teach. I have never spoken on my own authority. I know that the message my Father commanded reveals the way to eternal life. Because I know that, everything I say is my Father's command."

Prophecies About Jerusalem and the End Times
(Matthew 24:1–42; Mark 13:1–33; Luke 21:5–36)

As I was leaving the temple with my disciples, they were admiring the beautiful buildings of the temple with its carved stones and ornaments. They pointed these out to me. As we headed out to the Mount of Olives, I said to them, "See all these great buildings? The day is coming when there will not be one stone left on top of another. They will all be thrown down." I sat down when we got to the top of the Mount of Olives. My disciples gathered around and asked, "Tell us when this will happen. What will be the warning signs when this will happen? What do we look for when you are about to return at the end of the age?"

I began to answer them. "Be careful not to let anyone lead you astray. Many will come in my name proclaiming, 'I am the

Christ' and 'the time is near!' They will deceive many people. When you hear of wars and rumors of wars, don't be alarmed. These things must happen, but the end will not come yet. Many nations and kingdoms will make war with one another. There will be great earthquakes all over the world. Famines and plagues will be common, as will be frightening signs from heaven. All of this is only the beginning of suffering. Before all these things, they will grab hold of you and persecute you. They will bring you before councils and beat you in the synagogues and put you in prisons. You will represent me when you are brought before governors and kings, where you will testify in their presence. The gospel must first be preached to all nations. When you are taken to court don't worry about it. Settle it in your minds before these things happen that you are not going to waste time planning the right answers. Say whatever is given you when you stand there because it will not be just you who speak, it will be the Holy Spirit. He will give you answers with such great wisdom that none of your enemies will be able to stand against you or contradict your words.

"Families will be divided. Brother will turn over brother to the executioner. Even parents will turn you in. Children will betray their parents. Some of you will be put to death. You will be hated by everybody because you bear my name, but not a hair of your head will perish. Many will fall away when the heat is on; they will betray the faithful and hate one another. Many false prophets will appear and deceive thousands. Wickedness will multiply, causing many to lose the love they once had, but those who endure to the end will be saved. This gospel of the kingdom will be preached to all nations all over the world as a testimony, and then the end will come.

"When you see Jerusalem surrounded by armies and the desolating sacrilege, spoken of by the prophet Daniel,[69] standing in the holy place, then know that the end has come near. (Let the reader understand.) Those in Judea should flee to the mountains and anyone in the city should leave as fast as possible. If you are

---

[69] Daniel 11:31; 12:11

on your housetop, don't even go into the house to get anything. If you are in the field, don't go back to get your robe, for these are the days of revenge to fulfill all that has been written. How sad for those who are pregnant or those who have a baby at that time. Pray that you will not be escaping in winter or on the Sabbath. If the Lord hadn't shortened those days, no one would be saved. For the sake of the elect, his chosen, those days will be shortened. There will be great distress on the earth and wrath on this people. They will die by the sword and be led captive among all the nations. Jerusalem will be overrun by the nations until the times of the nations are fulfilled.

"Then if anyone says to you, 'Look, the Christ is here!' or 'There he is!' don't believe it. Many false Christs and false prophets will turn up, even showing great signs and wonders capable of fooling even the elect, if it were possible. Remember, I have warned you ahead of time. So if someone tells you, 'Come and see, he's in the wilderness,' don't bother to go there. If they say, 'We have found him in an inner room,' don't believe it. Just as the lightning shines from east to west, even so will the coming of the Son of Man be. Wherever the body is, that's where the vultures will gather.

"Right after the terrible times of those days, the sun and moon will become darkened. The stars will fall out of the sky. There will be great distress among the nations on earth; the sea will roar with great waves. People will collapse with dread because of what will be happening because even the powers in the sky will be shaken. Then the evidence of the Son of Man will appear in the sky and all the tribes of the earth will lament. They will see the Son of Man coming on the clouds with power and great glory. He will send out his angels to gather his chosen ones from all over the earth. When these things begin to happen, look up because your salvation is very close. Take a lesson from the fig tree. As soon as its branches start leafing out, you know summer is near. In the same way, when you see these things happening, you know the kingdom of God is near. This is certain: that generation shall not die off before all these events take place.

"Heaven and earth will cease to exist, but my words will last forever. But no one knows the day or hour, not even the angels in heaven or the Son. Only my Father knows the time of these events. The coming of the Son of Man will be just like the coming of the flood in the days of Noah. People were eating and drinking, marrying and giving in marriage until Noah went into the ark. They didn't have a clue until the flood drowned them all. Two men will be in the field; one will be taken, the other left. Two women will be grinding grain, one will be taken and the other left. Take care yourselves that you don't get careless under the stress of life. Don't get loaded down with over-indulging so that the day doesn't come on you like a trap. For that day will come on everyone living on the earth. Therefore, watch and pray, because you don't know when the Lord is coming. Pray for strength to escape the evil and all the things that will come, so that you will stand before the Son of Man."

Parables of the Second Coming
(Mark 13:34–37)

"My return is like a man who went on a long trip. When he left, he put his servants in charge, each with his own assignment. The doorkeeper was ordered to be always on the watch. You must be on the lookout at all times because you can never tell when your Master will return. It could be any time of the day or night. Don't let him catch you sleeping. My word to you is for all: Watch!"

(Matthew 25:1–13)

"The kingdom of God can be compared to ten maidens who took their lamps and went to meet the bridegroom. Five were foolish and five were wise. They all took their lamps, but the foolish had no oil in theirs. The wise put oil in their lamps and even took jars of extra oil. Because the bridegroom was delayed, they all fell asleep. At midnight, the announcement was heard, 'The bridegroom is coming! Come and meet him.' The maidens all woke up and trimmed their lamp wicks. The foolish said to the wise, 'Our lamps are going out. Give us some of your oil.' The wise answered, 'If we share our oil, we won't have enough either. You will have to go and buy some yourselves.' While they were gone buying oil, the bridegroom came. The wise virgins went in with him to the wedding feast. The door was shut. Eventually, the other maidens came knocking on the door, calling out, 'Lord, open the door for us.' He answered, 'Honestly, I don't know you.' Watch out, then, because you don't even know the day, nor the hour."

(Matthew 25:14–30)

"It will be the same as when a man goes away, leaving his property in the care of his servants. Knowing their abilities, he gives one five thousand dollars, another two thousand and a third, one thousand. The first goes right out, puts his money to work and gains five thousand more. The one with two thousand doubles his. But the one with one thousand buries it in a safe place. When the man returns, he settles up with them.

"The first comes forward, 'Master, you gave me five thousand dollars. See here, I have earned five thousand more.' His master replies, 'Very well done. You have been faithful with a little; I will entrust you with much. Come, share my joy.' The servant with the two thousand also comes, showing how he doubled it. The master says the same to him, 'Very well done, you have been faithful with a little; I will entrust you with much. Come, share my joy.' The servant with one thousand speaks, 'Master, I know you are a harsh man who expects to harvest what you didn't plant and to gather where you didn't sow. Here is your thousand. I hid it in the ground to keep if safe.' The master speaks, 'You wicked, lazy servant. So I harvest where I don't plant and gather where I don't sow? You should have at least put it in the bank so I gained interest. Take the thousand from him and give it to the one who has ten. To everyone who has, more will be given; he will have abundance. For him who hasn't anything, even what he has will be taken away. Throw the useless servant into outer darkness where men will grieve and grind their teeth.'"

(Matthew 25:31–46)

"When the Son of Man returns in all his majesty, accompanied by all the angels, he will sit on his magnificent throne. All the nations will be gathered in front of him. He will sort them out just like a shepherd removes the sheep from among the goats. He will put the sheep on his right hand and the goats on the left. Then the King will say to those on his right, 'Come, blessed by my Father—occupy the kingdom prepared for you since the world began. For I was starving and you fed me, I was thirsty and you brought me water, I was an alien and you included me in the family, I was naked and you dressed me, I was sick and you came and sat by my bed, I was in prison and you visited me.' Surprised, the righteous will ask, 'Lord, when did we ever see you starving and feed you? Or thirsty and bring you water? And when were you an alien and we included you? Or naked and dressed you? And when did we see you sick or in prison and visited you?' The King will explain, 'I tell you the truth, whatever you did for the poorest of my brothers and sisters, you did for me.'

"He will then turn to these on his left, 'Away from me, you who are now cursed, into the everlasting fire prepared for the devil and his angels. For I was starving and you didn't feed me, I was thirsty and you never brought water, I was an alien and you shut me out, I was naked and you never clothed me, I was sick and in prison and you never came near me.' They, too, will answer, 'Lord, when did we ever see you hungry or thirsty or an alien or naked or sick or imprisoned and did not minister to you?' Then the king will answer them, 'I tell you the truth, whatever you failed to do for the poorest of my brothers and sisters, you failed to do for me.' They will be sent away into everlasting punishment. The righteous will enter into eternal life."

(Matthew 26:1–2)

After I finished telling my disciples these parables, I said to them, "You know the Passover is only two days off. Then I will be betrayed and crucified."

The Betrayal
(Matthew 26:3–5; 14–16; Mark 14:1–2; 10–11; Luke 22:1–6)

With the Passover two days away, the chief priests and scribes gathered in the palace of Caiaphas, the high priest. They plotted how they could arrest and kill me quietly. They agreed, "We better not do it during the feast or we may have a riot on our hands."

Satan came to their aid. He entered into Judas Iscariot, one of the twelve disciples. Judas went to the chief priests to make a deal with them. He asked, "What will you give me if I deliver him to you?" They were delighted, so they paid him thirty pieces of silver, the price of a slave. From then on, Judas kept looking for an opportunity to betray me when the crowds were not there.

Passover Preparation
(Matthew 26:17–19; Mark 14:12–16; Luke 22:7–13)

It was Thursday, the first day of Unleavened Bread and the day the Passover lamb was sacrificed. So I sent Peter and John, telling them, "Go, prepare the Passover for us so we may celebrate it."

They asked me, "Where are we going to eat the Passover?"

I said, "Go into the city. A man carrying a jar of water will meet you. Follow him until he enters a house. Say to the householder, 'The Teacher says his time is at hand. Where is the guest room where the Passover is to be eaten with his disciples?' He will show you a large upper room already furnished. Prepare the meal there." They went into the city and found everything just as I had told them, so they prepared the Passover.

In the Upper Room

(Matthew 26:20–29; Mark 14:17–25; Luke 22:14–30; John 13:1–32)

I already knew before I went with my disciples to celebrate the feast of the Passover that the time for me to leave this world and go to my Father had come. I dearly loved those who were my own whom I had to leave here in this world. So when evening came, I went with my disciples to the upper room, my mind and heart heavy, knowing what they faced and how little they understood what I had to go through.

So I said to them, "I have longed to eat this Passover with you before I have to suffer. I assure you, I will never eat it again with you until everything is fulfilled in the kingdom of God." Then I took a cup of wine and gave thanks for it. I handed it to my disciples, saying, "Take this and divide it between yourselves. For my part, I will not drink the fruit of the vine until the kingdom of God comes."

When they came to take their places around the table, an argument started as to who was the greatest. So I said, "The kings of the nations lord it over everyone; those in authority even call themselves benefactors. But this is not the way it will be with you. The oldest among you must be on the same level as the youngest and the leader the same as the servant. Who is greater, the one who reclines at the table or the one who serves? Isn't it the one at the table? But among you, I am the same as one who serves.

"You are the ones who have walked with me through all my trials. Just as my Father has appointed a kingdom for me, I also appoint the same for you. You will eat and drink at my table in my kingdom and sit on thrones judging the twelve tribes of Israel."

At that point, I rose from the table, took off my cloak and tied up my remaining clothes with a towel. I poured water into a basin and began washing my disciple's feet and drying them with the towel around my waist. The disciples reclined in embarrassed silence until I came to Peter. It was too much for him, so he said, "Lord! You are going to wash my feet?"

I said to him, "What I am doing you do not understand now, but you will later on."

Pulling his feet up under him, Peter asserted, "You are never going to wash my feet!"

I replied with equal determination. "If I do not wash your feet, you will have no share in me."

Hearing that, Peter straightened out his legs. "Lord, don't stop with just my feet; wash my hands and my head too."

I said to him, "When a person has had a bath, he doesn't need to be washed again; except for his feet, he is clean all over. You are clean in this room, but not all of you." When I said, "Not all of you," I was referring to the one I knew was going to betray me.

When I finished washing their feet, I put my cloak back on and returned to my place at the table.

"Do you understand what I have done? You call me Teacher and Lord. You are right, for that is who I am. If I, your Lord and Teacher, have washed your feet, you should also wash one another's feet. I have given you an example—do just as I have done to you. I tell you, a servant is not greater than his master. A person who is sent is not greater than the one who sent him. If you remember these things, you will be blessed if you do them. I am not talking about all of you; I know whom I have chosen. But the Scriptures must be fulfilled, 'He who ate bread with me has turned against me.'[70] I tell you these things now, before they happen, so that when they do, you will know that I am the one I claimed to be. I solemnly affirm, whoever receives anyone I send receives me, and whoever receives me, receives the one who sent me."

As we reclined at the table eating, I became deeply troubled in my spirit. I had to come out with it. "This is the truth. One of you who is eating with me at this table is going to betray me. The way I go has been determined, but how terrible for the man who betrays me. It would have been better if he had never been born."

---

[70] Psalm 41:9

They all stopped eating as horror filled their faces. In sorrow, they looked at one another, none knowing what to say. Then, one after another, they said to me, "Is it I?"

I replied, "It is one of you who is dipping bread with me in the dish."

Judas asked, "Is it I, Master?"

I said to him, "It is as you have said."

John, one of my disciples whom I loved, was leaning against my chest. Peter signaled him across the table, whispering aloud, "Find out who he is referring to."

So John, leaning against me, whispered, "Lord who is it?"

I said, "It's the one I will give this piece of bread after I have dipped it." I gave the piece to Judas Iscariot, son of Simon. After he ate it, Satan entered into him. I said to Judas, "What you are going to do, do quickly." The others at the table didn't know why I said this. Because Judas kept the money bag, they thought I was telling him to buy what was needed for the feast or to give something to the poor. After I said this, Judas went out into the night.

When he had gone, I said, "The Son of Man is now glorified, and God is glorified in the Son. In himself, God will also glorify the Son, and he will do it at once."

As they were eating, I took a loaf, and when I had given thanks, I broke it and handed it to them. I said, "Take and eat; this is my body which is given for you. Do this in remembrance of me."

After supper, I took a cup. I gave thanks and passed it to them, saying, "Drink it, all of you. This is my blood of the new covenant, which is poured out for many for the forgiveness of sins. It is true that I shall not drink again of the fruit of the vine until the day when I drink it new with you in my Father's kingdom."

(Matthew 26:31–35; Mark 14:27–31; Luke 22:31–34; John 13:33–38)

"My little children, I am only with you for a little while. You will look for me. As you heard me say to the Jews, I say to you now: you cannot come where I am going. I am giving you a new commandment and this is it: love one another. You are to love one another in the same way that I have loved you. The fact you love one another will be the defining trait that will set you apart as belonging to me—by this all men will recognize you as my disciples."

Simon Peter said to me, "Lord, where are you going?"

I responded, "Right now you cannot follow me, but afterward you will follow." I then went on to say, "You will all abandon me because of this night. As it is written, 'I will strike the shepherd, and the sheep will be scattered.'[71] But after I am raised up, I will go before you to Galilee."

Peter broke in, "Even if everyone else abandons you, I never will."

I looked at him. "You will lay down your life for me? I must tell you, Peter, this is the truth: even before the rooster crows this morning, you will have denied me three times."

Peter responded very forcefully, "Even if I have to die with you, I will never deny you." The others all chimed in, saying the same thing.

I Am the Way
(John 14:1–31)

There was so much I wanted to tell them in the remaining few hours. So I began, "Don't let sorrow fill your hearts. You believe in God; then believe in me also. My Father's house has many places to live. If that were not true, I would have told you before now. I am going to get a place ready for you. The fact that I will get a place ready means I am coming back to take you to be with me. Wherever I will be, you will be with me too. You know the way to where I am going."

Thomas said to me, "Lord, we don't know where you are going, so how can we know the way?"

I replied, "I am the way, the truth and the life. No one can come to my Father except through me. If you have known me,

---

[71] Zechariah 13:7

you will have known my Father also. From now on you know him; you have seen him."

Philip spoke, "Lord, we will understand if you just show us the Father."

I said, "You have been with me so long, Philip. Don't you know me yet? Whoever has seen me has already seen my Father. How can you say, then, 'Show us the Father'? Don't you believe that I am in my Father and my Father is in me? None of the words I speak to you come from my own authority. They come from my Father who lives in me; he does his works through me. You must believe this: I am in my Father and my Father is in me. At least you must believe me because of the works you have seen me do.

"I tell you the truth: whoever has faith in me will be able to do the same works that I do. In fact, they will be able to do greater works than these because I am returning to my Father. I will do whatever you ask in my name so that my Father will be glorified in me. Anything you ask in my name I will do. This will happen because, if you love me, you will keep my commandments.

"I will ask my Father and he will send you another one who will encourage and defend you. He is the Spirit of truth and he will be with you forever. The world cannot accept him because it doesn't see him or know him. You do know him, because he lives with you and will be in you. I will not leave you as destitute orphans; I will come to you. In a little while the world won't see me, but you will certainly see me. Because I will continue to live, you will continue to live as well. In the days to come you will understand that I am in my Father, that you are in me, and I am in you. Anyone who loves me and has my commandments will keep them. My Father will love whoever loves me, and I will love them and reveal myself to them."

Judas (not Iscariot) said to me, "Lord, how come you will reveal yourself to us but not to the world?"

I answered him, "Anyone who loves me will keep my word, and my Father will love them as well. My Father and I will make our home with them. Those who do not love me don't obey my words, even though the words you hear me say are not mine but are the Father's who sent me.

"I have spoken these things to you while I am still here with you. But your helper, the Holy Spirit, will teach you everything—he's the one my Father will send in my name. He will remind you of everything I have told you. I give you peace. The peace I give you is my peace; the world has nothing to give you compared to it. So don't let trouble fill your hearts. Don't be afraid, either.

"You hear me tell you that I am going away and that I will come to you. If your love for me was complete, you would have been filled with joy for me because I go to my Father; he is greater than I. I have told you these things now, before they happen, so that you will believe when they do happen. I won't talk with you much longer because this world's ruler is coming. He has no power over me; what I will do is my Father's command to me. That way, the world will know how much I love my Father."

I Am the Vine
(John 15:1–27)

"I am the real vine and my Father is the gardener. He cuts off any of my branches that produce no fruit. He trims the fruit-bearing branches so they become even more fruitful. The teaching I have given you has already pruned you. Keep being one with me and I will stay one with you. A branch of a vine cannot bear fruit unless it is attached to the vine. Neither can you bear fruit unless you keep being one with me. I am the vine, the source of life for you, the branches. Clearly, those who bear much fruit continue being one with me and I with them, for without me, you can't do a thing. Those who think they know better than the vine and attempt to bear fruit of their own dry up; they become dead sticks which are thrown into the fire and burned. If you remain one with me and allow my words to continue with you, you can ask whatever you desire and I will do it for you. When you produce much fruit in your life, you glorify my Father and thus prove you really are my disciples.

"I have loved you with the same incredible love my Father has poured out on me. Bask in my love; don't ever walk away from it, even for a moment! If you continue to obey my commandments, you will always be surrounded with my love; you will be doing the same as I do as I obey my Father's commandments and bask in his love. I have said these things to you so that you will experience the fullness of my joy in your lives.

"My commandment is this: love one another with the same love I have poured out on you. The greatest love a person can have is to forfeit his life for his friends. You are my friends if you obey what I command you. I call you servants no longer, for a servant is not told what the master is up to. I call you friends because I have shared with you everything my Father has made known to me. In spite of what you may have thought, you didn't choose me—I chose you. I selected you and set you apart to bear much fruit. I have planned that your fruit would last, so that whatever you ask my Father for in my name, he will be able to give it to you. Let me repeat my command that enables you to bear fruit: love one another.

"Don't be surprised if the world hates you. After all, it hated me before it hated you. If you still lined up with the world's way of thinking, it would love you, for the world loves those who don't rock the boat. But you are forever changed because I chose you out of the world. You no longer fit in, so the world hates you. Remember what I already told you, 'A servant isn't greater than his master.' So if they persecuted me, they'll persecute you. If they took my word to heart, they will take yours also. They will do all this to you on account of me because they don't know my Father who sent me. If I hadn't come and told them the truth, they wouldn't be guilty of sin; now they have no excuse for their rebellion.

"Whoever hates me also hates my Father. If I hadn't done powerful works among them that no one else has ever done, they wouldn't be guilty of sin. Now they have witnessed these works and even so, they have hated both me and my Father. This fulfills what the Law says, 'They hated me without a cause.'[72] But when the Helper comes, whom I will send you from my Father—the Spirit of truth who comes from the Father—he will testify concerning me. You will also testify because you have been with me from the beginning of my ministry.

I Go—The Spirit Comes
(John 16:1–33)

"I have said all this to keep you from quitting because of what you will experience. They will throw you out of synagogues. The time is coming when people who kill you will think they are doing God a favor. They will do this because they don't know my Father or me. But because I've said these things, they will come to your mind when the time comes. I didn't tell you these things from the start because I was with you. But now I am returning to my Father who sent me and none of you asks me, 'Where are you going?'

"Hearing these things has filled your hearts with sorrow, but here is the truth you need to know. It is actually an advantage to you that I go away. If I don't go, the Helper won't come to you; if I do go, I will send him to you. When he comes, he will convince the world of the reality of sin, of uprightness and of judgment. About sin—because they refused to believe in me. About uprightness—because I am going to my Father and will not be visible to them anymore. About judgment—because Satan, who rules this world, is judged.

"There are many other things I would like to say to you, but they are more than you can handle right now. When the Spirit of truth comes, he will reveal the whole truth to you. He will not speak from his own authority; rather, he will speak only what he is told. He will tell you about many things that are yet to come and he will bring glory to me, for he will tell you what is mine. Everything of my Father's is mine; that's why I said he will tell

---

[72] Psalm 69:4

you what is mine. In a little while you won't see me anymore. Then, a little while longer, and you will see me."

Some of my disciples began saying to one another, "What is he trying to tell us? 'A little while and you won't see me. Then, a little while longer and you will see me,' And, 'Because I go to my Father'?" Some said, "What does he mean by, 'a little while'? We don't know what he means."

I knew they wanted to ask me, so I said to them, "Is this what you are wondering about: 'a little while you won't see me and a little while and you will see me'? I tell you the truth, you will mourn and cry while the world will rejoice. You will experience deep sorrow, but your sorrow will turn to joy. When a woman is in labor, she suffers, knowing the time has come. But when the baby is born, she forgets all the pain because of the joy of another child born into the world. In the same way, you will have sorrow now, but I will see you again and you will rejoice, a joy that no one will be able to take away from you.

"When that day comes, you will no longer ask any questions. I assure you, if you ask the Father for anything in my name, he will give it to you. Up until now you haven't asked for anything in my name, but now ask and your request will be granted that your joy may be complete. I have been speaking to you in figurative language. The time is soon coming when I won't do that anymore. I will tell you plainly about the Father. Then you will ask in my name. I'm not saying I shall pray to the Father on your behalf, because the Father loves you himself. He loves you because you have loved me and you have believed that I came from the Father. I came from the Father and came into the world, but now I am leaving the world and returning to the Father."

My disciples said, "Now you are speaking plainly, not in figurative language. We now understand that you do know all things, that there is no question about who you are. We believe you came from God."

I responded, "You really do believe now? The time is coming—in fact it has already come—when you will all be scattered, each to his home. You will all leave me alone; yet I am not alone because my Father is with me. I have told you this so you may be at peace in yourselves. You will have trials in the world, but cheer up, I have overcome the world."

Prayer to the Father
(John 17:1–26)

After I finished my last teaching with my disciples, I looked up to my Father in heaven, saying, "Daddy, my time has come. Magnify your Son that your Son may be able to magnify you. You have given me power over all humanity to give eternal life to all those you have given to me. This is life forever: to know you, the only God who actually lives, and to know me, Jesus, the Christ whom you sent. I have magnified you on earth; I have finished the work you gave me to do. Now, Daddy, glorify me in your presence with the same glory I had with you before the world was created.

"I have made your name well known to the men you gave me from out of the world. They were yours and you gave them to me. They have obeyed your word. They know now that everything I have been given comes from you. They have received the gift of my words, all of them given to me by you. They also know the profound truth that I came from you; they have recognized that you are the one who sent me.

"I am not praying for the world. This, my prayer, is for those you have given me, for they are yours. All these that are mine are also completely yours; all these that are yours are also completely mine. It is in them that I am glorified. I'm not going to be in the world in the flesh now, but they are going to continue on in the world. I am coming home to you. Holy Father, keep them united in the power of the name which you chose for me—may they be one just the same as we are one. While I have been with them in the name which you gave me, I have protected them. None are lost except the son of destruction, the fulfillment of Scripture.

"Now I am soon coming to you, so I am saying these things while I am still in this world so that my joy will rest upon them, filling their own hearts and lives even though I am gone. I have given them your word so they are no longer part of the world. The world now hates them because they are no more part of the world than I am. I am not praying for you to take them out of the world; I am asking that you protect them from the evil one. Since they are no more part of the world than I am, set them apart by the word of truth; your word is the truth that sets them apart. Just as you sent me into the world, I am sending them into the world. Therefore, I dedicate myself to the truth for their sakes so they will also be dedicated to the truth.

"My prayer is not only for those here now; it is also for all those who are going to believe in me because of your word which these will spread. Again, I pray that they will all be one in the same way that you, Daddy, are one with me and I am one with you. So, then, they also are one with us. By this the world will believe you have sent me. I am also giving them the glory that you have given me so that they may be one in glory even as we are one in glory—I in them and you in me. I pray that they will experience perfect oneness, which will prove to the world you sent me and that I love them even as you love me.

"Daddy, my deep desire is that all those you have given me will be with me where I will be so they may see my glory which you have given me, the glory your great love poured out on me before the world was ever created. Oh, glorious Father of righteousness, the world has never known you, but I have always known you. These know you sent me. I have revealed your name to them; I will continue to reveal it. Then the love which you have poured out on me will be in them also."

Gethsemane
(Matthew 26:30, 36–46; Mark 14:26, 32–42; Luke 22:35–46; John 18:1)

We sang a hymn as we prepared to go out. I said to them, "When I sent you out without a purse, bag or sandals, were you ever short of anything?"

They replied, "No, nothing at all."

I went on, "But now I tell you, if you have a purse take it with you. Do the same with a bag if you have one. If you don't have a sword, sell your mantle and buy one. The Scripture must be fulfilled regarding me, 'and he was classed as an outlaw.'[73] All that has been written about me will be fulfilled."

They said, "Here, Lord, we have two swords."

I said to them "That is enough." Then we went out into the night. As I often did, we went to the Mount of Olives, where there was a garden called Gethsemane.

When we arrived, I said to my disciples, "Sit here and pray that you will not give in to temptation. I am going over there to pray."

I took Peter, James and John with me. Extreme sorrow swept over me. I felt dizzy. My heart beat wildly. I stopped and said to them, "My soul is desolate. I feel like I am dying. Stay here and keep watch with me."

I staggered on about a stone's throw and collapsed on the ground, praying in desperation, "Daddy, everything is possible for you. Take this cup away from me!" I paused. "No, Daddy! Your will must be done, not mine."

At that point an angel appeared and strengthened me. I was in agony. My body shook all over and I began to sweat profusely. The moisture fell on the ground in huge drops mixed with blood. I was still shaky as I stood up. I walked back to my disciples, but they were all asleep; the sorrow was too much for them. I said to them, "Couldn't you watch with me for one hour? You need to watch and pray so temptation doesn't overcome you. Your spirits are willing but your flesh will be your downfall."

I returned to pray again, repeating essentially what I had prayed before. "Daddy, if there is no way I can avoid drinking this bitter cup, I will drink it, for your will must be done." I returned to my disciples again. They opened their heavy eyelids enough to see I was there, but they didn't even manage to say anything. They didn't know what to say. I went away a third

---

[73] Isaiah 53:12

time, praying similarly as before. Finally, my battle was over. I strode back to my disciples, "You are still sleeping? Stop resting, for the time has arrived. I have already been betrayed into evil hands. Get up and let's get going. The betrayer is nearly here."

Judas' Kiss
(Matthew 26:47–56; Mark 14:43–52; Luke 22:47–54; John 18:2–12)

Judas well knew where we were, for I often went to the garden with my disciples. I had scarcely aroused my disciples when he turned up with half an army—Roman soldiers and temple police, all armed with swords and clubs and carrying lanterns and torches. Judas was out in front, leading them. He had given the mob a sign, saying, "The one I kiss is the man you want. Seize him."

I was ready for them, so I walked up to them and asked, "Who are you looking for?"

Someone answered, "Jesus of Nazareth."

I said, "That's who I am." Startled, they stepped back and fell down on the ground.

Again I said, "Who are you looking for?"

Again the answer, "Jesus of Nazareth."

"I told you that's who I am, so let these other men go." This was to fulfill my word, "I did not lose one of those you gave me."

At this point Judas came up to me, saying, "Hail, Master!" Then he kissed me.

I said to him, "Judas, you would betray the Son of Man with a kiss?"

Then they came up and grabbed me. One of my disciples asked, "Lord, shall we use the swords?"

Peter carried one of the swords, so he came and hit Malchus, the slave of the high priest, cutting off his ear. I said to Peter, "Put your sword away, for everyone who trusts in the sword dies by the sword. I must drink the cup my Father has given me. Don't you know that I could appeal to my Father and he would immediately send me more than twelve legions of angels?" I then touched Malchus' ear and it was restored.

I turned to speak to the chief priests, elders and temple captains who came with the mob. "Who do you think you are coming to get? A dangerous robber? I was with you day after day, teaching in the temple, and you never laid a hand on me. But this is your hour, the power of darkness. The Scriptures must be fulfilled." The soldiers and the temple police tied me up securely. My disciples all ran away in terror. One young man who followed me had only a linen cloth on. They tried to seize him but he left his linen cloth behind and ran away naked.

Before the Chief Priests and the Council
(Matthew 26:57–68; Mark 14:53–65; Luke 22:54–55, 63–65; John 18:13–24)

They took me to Annas, the leader of the high priests, even though Caiaphas, his son-in-law was the official high priest that year. My disciple John followed the procession as they took me to the palaces of the high priest. Peter followed too, at a distance. John was able to enter the courtyard of the palaces because he was known to the high priest. Peter stood at the gate. When John saw him, he spoke to the maid who guarded the door and she let him in. It was cold, so the servants and officers lit a charcoal fire in the middle of the courtyard to warm themselves. Peter sat among them, warming himself.

Meanwhile, Annas questioned me about my disciples and my teaching. I responded, "There are no secrets about my teaching. I have spoken everything openly to the world. I have always spoken in synagogues and the temple where all the Jews gather. Why, then, do you ask me? Ask those who heard me; they know what I said."

After I said this, an officer standing there slapped me on the face, saying, "Is that how you reply to the high priest?"

His action was illegal, so I replied to him, "If what I said was improper, you have the right to testify to that fact. But if what I said was proper and truthful, on what basis did you strike me?"

Annas then sent me over to Caiaphas. The chief priests, elders and scribes had all gathered by this time. Caiaphas and the entire council tried to bring witnesses against me, giving them an excuse to put me to death. There was no shortage of false witnesses, but none of their testimonies agreed with one another. Finally, two of them came forward, declaring, "This man said, 'I will destroy this temple of God and in three days build another not made with hands.'" But even on this story, their testimony didn't agree.

Then the high priest stood up, "Don't you have any answer? What are these men testifying about who speak against you?" I refused to answer, so I remained silent. The high priest then said to me, "I charge you, in the name of the living God, tell us whether you are the Christ, the Son of God."

"I am, and I tell you, in the future you will see the Son of Man sitting at the right hand of power and coming on the clouds of heaven."

The high priest tore his robes, saying, "He has spoken blasphemy. Why do we need more witnesses? You have heard his blasphemy. What do you think?"

They answered, "He deserves death."

Then those standing there began spitting in my face and beating me. They covered my face, saying, "Prophecy to us, you Christ. Who hit you?" The guards also treated me with contempt as they beat on me.

Peter's Denial
(Matthew 26:69–75; Mark 14:66–72; Luke 22:56–62; John 18:25–27)

During this time, as Peter was sitting in the courtyard, one of the high priest's maids looked at him and said, "You were with Jesus, the Galilean."

Peter was caught off guard so he blurted out, "I don't know what you mean."

They all heard her, so he got up and walked toward the gate. Another maid recognized him and said to those standing there, "This man was with Jesus of Nazareth."

This time Peter used an oath and said, "I do not know the man!"

About an hour later, some bystanders came to Peter: "You certainly are one of them. Your Galilean accent gives you away."

A relative of the man Peter cut the ear off also spoke, "Didn't I see you in the garden with him?"

Peter began to curse and swear. "I don't know the man you are talking about."

Immediately the rooster crowed and I turned and looked at Peter. He saw the expression on my face and remembered that I had said, "Before the rooster crows, you will deny me three times." Completely broken, he rushed out of there, weeping bitterly.

Before the Sanhedrin
(Matthew 27:1; Mark 15:1; Luke 22:66–71)

As it was illegal under Jewish law to condemn anyone to death in a nighttime trial, they waited until dawn to formally assemble the entire council. They led me away to the council chambers, where the council had gathered along with the chief priests and scribes. They discussed together their plot to put me to death. Then they addressed me directly: "If you are the Christ, then tell us."

I said to them, "If I tell you, you won't believe; if I ask questions, you won't answer. But be assured of this, from now on the Son of Man will be seated in power at the right hand of the God of power."

They asked, "Are you the Son of God, then?"

I replied, 'It is as you say. I am."

Then they said, "We don't need any further testimony. We have heard ourselves from his own mouth."

Judas' Fate
(Matthew 27:3–10; Acts 1:16–20)

When Judas saw that I was condemned, he repented. He brought the thirty pieces of silver back to the chief priests and elders, saying, "I have sinned because I betrayed innocent blood."

They replied, "What do we care? That's your problem." Judas threw the pieces of silver into the temple and walked out.

He went from there and hung himself. The rope broke so that he fell to the ground and his intestines flowed out.

The chief priests picked up the silver, saying, "We cannot lawfully put this money in the treasury because it is blood money." They discussed the matter and decided to buy the potter's field where Judas died as a place to bury strangers in. Ever since, it has been called the Field of Blood. This fulfilled what Zechariah wrote: "And they took the thirty pieces of silver, the price that I was valued at by the children of Israel, and threw them to the potter in the house of the Lord."[74]

Before Pilate
(Matthew 27:2, 11–14; Mark 15:1–5; Luke 23:1–6; John 18:28–38)

The entire company in the council chambers rose up to take me to Pilate. They tied me up again before they took me to the Praetorium before Pilate. However, they wouldn't enter the Praetorium themselves because they would be defiled; they wanted to eat the Passover. So Pilate came out to them, asking, "What is the charge you bring against this man?"

They responded, "If this man wasn't doing evil we wouldn't have brought him to you."

Pilate turned it back to them, "Take him yourselves, then, and judge him according to your own law."

The Jews objected, "We cannot lawfully put anyone to death." This was to fulfill what I had said about how I would die.

Then they began to accuse me. "We have discovered this man perverting our nation. He forbids giving taxes to Caesar, saying that he is himself Christ, a king."

Pilate went back into the courtroom and called for me to be brought before him. "Are you the King of the Jews?"

I answered, "Do you ask me this for your own information or are you asking because others say this about me?"

Pilate replied, "Am I a Jew? Your own people and your chief priests have handed you over to me. What have you done?"

---

[74] Zechariah 11:13

I said, "My kingdom is not part of this world. If it was, my subjects would fight to deliver me from the Jews. As it is, my kingdom does not arise from this world."

Then Pilate said, "So you are a king, then?"

Again I answered, "You have asked if I am a king. Yes, for this reason I have come into the world. I have come to reveal the truth. Everyone who truly desires the truth hears my voice."

Pilate remarked, "What is truth?" Having said this, he went outside again to the Jews. "I cannot find any evidence of criminal intent in this man." The chief priests and the elders launched into a tirade of accusations against me.

Pilate returned to me, "Don't you hear all the things they accuse you of?"

I stood in silence, refusing to answer even a single charge. Pilate was amazed at my silence, but the leaders became even more vocal. "He stirs up the people with his teachings all through Judea, beginning in Galilee all the way here to this city. When Pilate heard Galilee mentioned, he asked if I was a Galilean. When he found this out, he realized I belonged to Herod's jurisdiction, so he sent me over to Herod, who happened to be in Jerusalem at the time.

Before Herod
(Luke 23:7–12)

When Herod saw me, he was pleased because he had wanted to see me for a long time. He had heard a lot about me so he hoped to see me do some miracle. He questioned me for some time but I refused to even say a word to him. The chief priests and scribes had come along, still making all kinds of accusations against me. Herod and his soldiers treated me contemptuously. They made a mockery of me, putting a gorgeous robe on me and sending me back to Pilate. That day Pilate and Herod became friends. Up until then they had been enemies.

Back to Pilate

(Matthew 27:15–31; Mark 15:6–20; Luke 23:13–25; John 18:39–19:16)

Pilate called the chief priests and rulers of the people back before him. "You brought this man to me, claiming he was perverting the people. I have examined him before you. I cannot find him guilty of any of the charges you made against him. Herod did not find anything either. That is why he sent him back. He has done nothing worthy of death."

It was the custom at the Passover feast for the governor to release one prisoner. The people could ask for anyone they wanted. Among the prisoners in the jail was a well-known man called Barabbas, who was guilty of murder in an insurrection. The crowd came up to Pilate, asking that he release one prisoner at the feast as the custom was.

Pilate could see that I was brought before him because the chief priests were jealous. His wife had also sent a warning to him, "Have nothing to do with that righteous man; I have suffered extreme pain over him in a dream this morning." So Pilate, wanting to release me, said, "Do you want me to release to you the King of the Jews?"

The chief priests had persuaded the people to ask for Barabbas, so when Pilate asked this, they shouted, "Away with this man! Release Barabbas to us."

Then Pilate asked, "What shall I do, then, with this man whom you call the King of the Jews?"

They all began shouting, "Crucify him! Crucify him!"

Again Pilate spoke, "Why? What evil has he done? I don't find any crime in him worthy of death. I will therefore scourge him and let him go." Pilate went back into the courtroom and ordered me scourged. After this the soldiers took me into the courtroom and, gathering the whole battalion, stripped me of my clothes and put a scarlet robe on me. They plaited a crown of thorns and put it on my head and a reed in my hand. They knelt before me and mocked me, saying, "Hail, King of the Jews!" They hit me with their hands and spat on me.

Pilate went out again to the crowd. "Look, I'm bringing him out to you so you may know I find no crime in him." So I came out, wearing the purple robe and the crown of thorns. Pilate proclaimed, "Here is the man!"

When the chief priests and the officers saw me, they shouted, "Crucify him! Crucify him!"

Pilate said, "Take him yourselves and crucify him, because I find no reason for him to suffer the death penalty."

The Jews answered, "We have a law, and according to that law he should die because he has declared himself the Son of God."

When Pilate heard that he was even more frightened. So he went back into the courtroom with me and asked, "Where are you from?" I didn't say a word, so he continued, "You won't speak to me? Don't you know that I have the power to release you or to crucify you?"

So I answered him, "You wouldn't have any power over me at all if it hadn't been given to you from above. For that reason, the one who delivered me to you has the greatest sin."

Pilate tried to release me, but the Jews called out, "If you release this man, you're no friend of Caesar; anyone who makes himself king is an enemy of Caesar."

Hearing these words, Pilate brought me out again. He sat down on the judge's seat at a place called The Pavement—in Hebrew, Gabbatha. It was the day of preparation for the Passover and it was around noon. He said to the Jews, "Here is your king!"

They just shouted all the more, "Let him be crucified! Crucify him!"

Pilate replied, "Shall I crucify your king?"

The chief priests answered, "We have no king but Caesar!"

When Pilate saw that he was getting nowhere and that a riot was about to begin, he took water and washed his hands in front of them all. As he did so, he said, "I am innocent of this man's blood; you look after it yourselves."

All the people responded, "His blood be upon us and on our children!" Their shouting prevailed, so Pilate pronounced the sentence they demanded and released Barabbas to them. The soldiers took the scarlet robe off and put my own clothes back on me.

The Crucifixion
(Matthew 27:31–56; Mark 15:20–41; Luke 23:26–49; John 19:17–30)

The soldiers then led me away to be crucified. I was forced to carry my own cross, as was the custom. As we were leaving the city, they seized a man named Simon from Cyrene,[75] the father of Alexander and Rufus. He happened to be coming in from the country. They forced him to carry my cross behind me. A large crowd followed, including many women who cried out, overcome with grief. I turned to them and said, "Daughters of Jerusalem, don't weep for me. You need to weep for yourselves and for your children because the days are coming when people will say, 'Most blest are the childless, the empty wombs, the dry breasts.' In that day, they will cry to the mountain, 'Fall on us,' to the hills, 'Bury us.' If they do this when the wood is green, what will happen when it is dry?"

Two criminals were led away to be crucified with me. Eventually, we came to Skull Hill—in Hebrew, Golgotha. They offered me wine mixed with myrrh to drink, but when I tasted it, I wouldn't drink it. There I was crucified along with the criminals, one on each side. As they did this I prayed, "Daddy, forgive them; they have no idea what they are doing."

Pilate had a sign written and hung on my cross. It stated, "Jesus of Nazareth, King of the Jews." It was written in Hebrew, Latin and Greek. Many Jews read it because the place where I was crucified was close to the city. The chief priests complained to Pilate, "Don't write, 'The King of the Jews.' Rather put, 'This man said, 'I am the King of the Jews.'"

Pilate dismissed their complaint with, "What I have written, I have written."

---

[75] North Africa

After I was hung on the cross, the soldiers divided up my clothes into four parts, one for each soldier. But when they came to my coat, they discovered it was made without a seam, woven in one piece from top to bottom. They said to one another, "We shouldn't tear this, so let's throw dice to see who gets it." Even this fulfilled the Scripture, "They divided up my clothes between them and threw dice for my coat."[76]

The people stood around watching, but the Jewish rulers and the chief priests ridiculed me, saying, "He saved other people. Let's see if he can save himself, for he claimed to be the Christ of God, his Chosen One. He trusts in God, so let God rescue him now if he wants him. Let him come down from the cross, then we will believe in him."

The soldiers even joined in, coming to me and offering vinegar and saying, "If you are the King of the Jews, save yourself!"

Others passing by also ridiculed. They wagged their heads, saying, "Ha! You who would destroy the temple and build it in three days, why don't you save yourself and come down from the cross?"

One of the criminals hanging with me joined in. "Aren't you the Christ? Save yourself and us too."

But the other criminal rebuked him. "Don't you even fear God, you who are also hanging here under the same sentence? We are being justly punished for the deeds we have done, but this man has done nothing wrong."

Then he spoke to me. "Jesus, remember me when you come into your kingdom."

I said to him, "I assure you, today you will be with me in Paradise."

Standing by the cross was my mother and her sister. Also there were Mary, the wife of Clopas, and Mary Magdalene. Seeing my mother standing there beside John, I said to her, "Woman, look at your son!" To John, I said, "See! Your mother!" From that time, John took her home to his own house.

---

[76] Psalm 22:18

From noon to about three o'clock, the whole land was enveloped in darkness. Around three o'clock, out of the desolation of my spirit, I shouted, "Eloi, Eloi, lama sabachthani?" which means, "My God, my God, why have you forsaken me?"

Some of those standing around thought I was calling Elijah. Others said, "Wait, let's see if Elijah will come and take him down."

Nearing my last breath, I said, "I'm thirsty." There was a bowl of vinegar standing there, so someone soaked a sponge in it and held it to my mouth on the end of a reed.

I quietly said, "It is finished," then, with a final burst of energy, I shouted, "Daddy, into your hands I commit my spirit!" Having said that, I bowed my head and gave up my spirit.

At that moment, the curtain of the temple was ripped apart from top to bottom. There was a violent earthquake, the rocks split and tombs were opened. Many bodies of the saints who had died came out of the tombs and went into the city, appearing to many people. When the centurion and those keeping watch over me with him saw the earthquake and all that happened, they were awestruck. The centurion praised God, saying, "Surely this was a Son of God. This man was innocent." All the crowds who had come to see what took place were also moved. They went to their homes, beating their breasts along the way. There were also many women there who had ministered to me while I was in Galilee and who had come to Jerusalem with me. Among those who witnessed my death were Mary Magdalene and Mary, the mother of James and Joseph. Also present were the mother of the sons of Zebedee and Salome.

My Burial
(Matthew 27:57–61; Mark 15:42–47; Luke 23:50–56; John 19:31–42)

As this all happened on the day of Preparation, the day before the Sabbath, the Jewish leaders did not want the bodies left on the crosses on the Sabbath, especially since this Sabbath was a special high day. So they asked Pilate to break the legs of those on the crosses so they would die and then be taken away.

When the soldiers came, they broke the legs of the two who had been crucified with me, but when they came to my body, they saw that I was already dead. As a result, they didn't need to break my legs, but one of them thrust a spear up into my side and immediately a flow of blood and water came out. The one who witnessed this told the truth so that doubting people would believe in my death. These things happened that the Scripture might be fulfilled, "Not a bone of his body shall be broken."[77] Another Scripture states, "They will look on me whom they have pierced."[78]

As evening approached, a rich man from Arimathea named Joseph, a respected member of the council, had the courage to ask Pilate for my body. He was a righteous man who searched for the kingdom of God and who had no part in what was done to me. He had remained a secret disciple for fear of the Jews. Pilate was surprised to hear I was already dead, so he called in a centurion to find out if it was true. When he was told I was dead, he granted Joseph the right to take my body. Joseph bought a linen shroud to wrap me in. He was joined by Nicodemus, also a member of the council, who had previously come to me by night. He brought with him a mixture of myrrh and aloes weighing around one hundred pounds. Together they wrapped me in the linen shroud along with the spices, as was the Jewish custom.

There was a garden near where I was crucified, and in it was a new rock-hewn tomb which had never been used. They laid me in there and rolled the huge stone across the entrance because they had little time before the Sabbath was to begin. Some of the women from Galilee followed along so they would know where I was buried. Their number included Mary Magdalene and Mary, the mother of Joses. These went and prepared spices and ointments. Then everyone rested on the Sabbath, as the commandments required.

---

[77] Psalm 34:20
[78] Zechariah 12:10

Guards at the Tomb
(Matthew 27:62–66)

The next day, on the Sabbath, the chief priests and the Pharisees gathered in front of Pilate, saying, "Sir, we remember how this pretender said while he was alive, 'After three days I will rise again.' Because of that, we want the tomb secured until the third day so his disciples cannot come and steal him away and then tell the people, 'He has risen from the dead' so the last pretense will be worse than the first."

By then Pilate had seen enough of them, so he wearily responded, "Okay. You have the soldiers—go and do what you can." So on a high Sabbath, they went with the soldiers and put a seal on the stone.

Resurrection
(Matthew 28:1–15; Mark 16:1–11; Luke 24:1–12; John 20:1–18)

While it was still dark, Mary Magdalene, Mary, mother of James, and Salome began walking toward the tomb, carrying the spices they had prepared. They began discussing with one another, "Who will roll the stone away for us?" They knew how huge it was.

At the crack of dawn there was a great earthquake as an angel of God descended from heaven and rolled the stone back. Then he sat on it. His face was like lightning and his clothing was a dazzling white. The guards shook in their boots, paralyzed with fear. They were like dead men.

Not long after, the women arrived. They were astonished to see the stone already rolled away. As soon as Mary Magdalene saw this, she left the others and ran to Simon Peter and John, telling them, "The stone is rolled away from the tomb! Someone must have taken the Lord out of the tomb and we don't know where they put him."

Meanwhile, the other women approached the tomb and saw the angel. He said to them, "Don't be afraid; I know you have come to see Jesus, who was crucified. He isn't here. He has risen just as he said he would. Come, see the place where he was laid." So they entered the tomb and saw that my body was not there.

Suddenly, two men stood by them, dressed in brilliant, shining clothes. The women bowed down with their faces touching the ground. They said to the women, "Why do you seek the living in the place of the dead? Remember what he told you while he was still in Galilee? He said that the Son of Man must be handed over to sinful men and be crucified and then he would rise on the third day. You go and tell Peter and his disciples that he is going to Galilee. You will see him there. Remember what we have told you." When they disappeared, the women ran from the tomb, trembling and afraid, and yet filled with great joy. They went to tell the disciples.

Peter and John ran to the tomb to check out Mary's story. Though John outran Peter, he stopped short, standing outside looking in. He stooped to see the linen cloths lying there. Peter, on the other hand, went past John and walked right into the tomb. He saw the linen cloths lying there with the head cloth rolled up separately by itself. John then followed Peter in, and seeing all this, believed the truth. They did not yet understand the Scripture that I must rise from the dead. Then the disciples went back to their homes.

Mary Magdalene returned to the tomb where she stood, just outside, crying. After a while she ventured to peak in, and when she did, she saw two angels in white, sitting one at the head and one at the foot of the place where I had lain. They said to her, "Woman, why are you crying?"

She answered, "It's because they took away my Lord, and I don't know where they put him." After saying this, she turned around and saw me standing there. It never even occurred to her that it was really me, so she just assumed I must be the gardener.

I quietly said, "Woman, why are you weeping? Who are you looking for?"

Through her tears, she pleaded, "Sir, if you have carried him away, tell me where you put him. I will take him away myself."

I said just one word.

"Mary."

She knew no one else ever said her name like that! She turned and looked at me, the tears still on her face now mingled with tears of ecstasy. She almost bounced with joy,

"Rabboni!"[79]

She was about to reach out to me when I spoke again, "Don't hold me, Mary, because I have not even ascended to my Father yet. Go to my brothers and tell them I am ascending to my Father and your Father, to my God and your God."

Later, I met the other women as they were returning from the tomb. I said, "Hail!" and with joy they knelt down and clasped my feet, worshipping me. I told them, "Don't be afraid. Tell my brothers to go to Galilee, for they will see me there." When the women told the disciples that they had actually seen me, they didn't believe them; to them it sounded like a fairytale.

Early in the morning while these events took place, some of the guards went into the city and told the chief priests all that had happened. The priests gathered with the elders to decide what to do. They paid the soldiers bribes to lie about what happened. "Tell people his disciples came during the night while you were sleeping and stole his body. If the governor hears about this, we will satisfy him and keep you out of trouble." So they took the money and did as they were told. This story was broadcast among the Jews for some time.

The Emmaus Road
(Mark 16:12; Luke 24:13–33)

On this same Sunday, two of my disciples left Jerusalem to go to the village of Emmaus about seven miles away. They were discussing all the events that had happened when I came alongside them on the road. Prevented their eyes from recognizing me, I asked them, "What is all this you are talking about along the road?"

They stopped, faces downcast, and one of them named Cleopas spoke up. "You must be the only visitor to Jerusalem

---

[79] Hebrew for "teacher."

these days who doesn't know about all the things that happened there."

I asked, "And to what things do you refer?"

He continued, "We are talking about Jesus of Nazareth, who was a powerful prophet, not only in what he said, but in the wonderful deeds he did as well. He did this before God and in the sight of all the people. But our chief priests and rulers had him condemned to death and crucified. We had understood him to be the one to redeem Israel."

The other said, "It is now the third day since this happened. Some women in our group went to the tomb early this morning, but they didn't find his body. They came back saying they saw angels who told them he was alive. Two of our men went to the tomb and found it empty but they didn't see him."

As we continued on I said, "Foolish men who are so slow to understand all that the prophets have said—wasn't it necessary for the Christ to suffer all these things and to then enter his glory?" So I began with Moses and the Prophets, interpreting to them all the things said about me throughout the Scriptures.

When we came near to Emmaus, I acted as though I was going on further, but they said to me, "Stay with us. It's getting too late to go further, for the day is nearly over." So I went into the house with them. When we sat at their table, I took the bread and gave thanks for it. Then I broke it before I handed it out to them. When I did this their eyes were opened and they recognized me. Before they could do or say anything, I vanished from sight.

As they looked at each other, joy spread over their faces. They agreed, "Wasn't there a fire in our hearts while he talked along the road, so clearly explaining the Scriptures to us?" They were far too excited to stay there; they had to tell their wonderful experience to the rest, so they rushed out the door to return to Jerusalem.

The Upper Room[80]
(Mark 16:13–14; Luke 24: 33–43; John 20:19–29)

On the evening of the resurrection Sunday, the disciples were gathered together with the doors locked in case the Jews might come looking for them. Ten of them were gathered there along with others when the two from Emmaus arrived. The disciples said to them, "The Lord really has risen. He has appeared to Simon!" Then the two from Emmaus told their story of the journey along the road and how they recognized me when I broke bread.

While they were reporting this, I came and stood among them. I said, "Peace be with you." They were not prepared for my appearance so they were frightened, thinking they were seeing a spirit. I reassured them, "Why are you upset and questioning in your hearts? See my hands and my feet; put your hands on me. A spirit doesn't have flesh and bones as you can see I have." After saying this, I held out my hands and showed them my feet and my side. It still seemed too good to be true for them as they wondered how this could be, yet they were filled with joy at the same time.

To further reassure them, I asked if they had something to eat. They gave me a piece of broiled fish and I ate it right there in front of them. I chided them for their unbelief—for not believing the women who saw me that morning just after I rose from the grave. Knowing their task was about to begin, I said, "My peace is with you. Just as the Father sent me, I am sending you." Then I breathed on them, saying, "Receive the Holy Spirit. If you forgive anyone's sins, they are forgiven; if you choose not to forgive the sins of anyone, they are not forgiven."

Thomas was not there that evening when I appeared, so the others told him, "We saw the Lord."

He was unconvinced, so he said, "Unless I see the nail-prints in his hands and put my finger on them and I put my hand in his side, I will not believe." Eight days later, when they gathered

---

[80] Acts 1:13

along with Thomas, once more with the doors locked, I again stood among them, saying, "Peace be with you." Then I turned to Thomas and, holding my hands out, said, "Put your finger here; see my hands. Put your hand in my side. Quit being faithless. Believe."

Thomas didn't need to touch me. He exclaimed, "My Lord and my God!"

I said, "Is it because you have seen me that you believe? More blest are those who have not seen me and believe just the same."

On the Shore of the Sea of Galilee
(John 21:1–23)

The next time my disciples saw me was on the shore of the Sea of Galilee, also called the Sea of Tiberias. Seven of them were gathered there: Simon Peter; Thomas, called the Twin; Nathanael of Cana in Galilee; James and John, sons of Zebedee; and two others.

Peter said, "I'm going fishing."

The others said, "We'll go with you."

They were out in the boat all night but never caught a thing. Just as the eastern sky was lighting up, they saw a figure on the beach. They didn't know it was me, so I called out, "Children, have you any fish?"

They called back, "No!"

So I called again, "Throw the net in on the right side of the boat and you'll find some."

Nothing else had worked, but they threw the net in anyhow. Suddenly, they realized they couldn't even pull the net in, there were so many fish. John said to Peter, "It's the Lord!" Hearing that, Peter threw on some clothes and jumped into the lake. They were only a hundred yards from shore, so the rest brought the boat in, dragging the bulging net along with them.

When they came ashore, they saw a charcoal fire with fish laying on it and bread to eat. I said to them. "Bring some of the fish you caught." Peter hauled the net up on shore; it was full of large fish. They counted one hundred and fifty-three of them. Amazingly, the net did not break. I said, "Come and have breakfast."

None of them dared ask me, "Who are you?" They knew in their hearts it was me. I gave them the bread and the fish. This was my third appearance to my disciples as a group since my resurrection.

When they had finished breakfast, I said to Peter, "Simon, son of John, are you more devoted to me than to these?"

Peter answered, "Yes, Lord, you know that I love you tenderly."

So I said, "Feed my lambs."

I asked him again, "Simon, son of John, are you really devoted to me?"

Peter replied as before, "Yes, Lord, you know that I love you tenderly."

I said, "Shepherd my sheep."

For a third and final time, I asked him, "Simon, son of John, do you really tenderly love me?"

Peter was deeply troubled that I asked him a third time so he said, "Lord you know everything. You know how much I tenderly love you."

I again replied, "Shepherd my sheep. I must say this to you. When you were young, you tied up your robe and walked wherever you wanted, but when you get old, you will stretch out your arms for someone else to tie up your robe and take you where you don't want to go." I said this to reveal by what death he was going to glorify God.

After this, I said to him, "Follow me." We were walking along the beach as I said this.

Peter heard someone behind us so he turned and saw John. Peter asked, "What about him?"

I replied, "What difference does that make to you? If I planned for him to live until I returned, so what? You just follow me." The rumor spread around that John was never going to die, but that was not what I said. I only said, "If I choose to let him live until I return, what difference does it make to you?"

Mountain in Galilee
(Matthew 28:16–20; Mark 16:15–18)

I directed my eleven disciples to meet me on a mountain in Galilee. After they had gathered, I came to them. When they saw me, they immediately fell down and worshipped me. I said to them, "I have been given all authority both in heaven and on earth. Make disciples of all nations, baptizing them in the name of the Father and of the Son and of the Holy Spirit. Teach them to carry out all I have commanded you. Be sure of this: I am always with you, right up to the end of the age."

Final Appearance and Ascension
(Luke 24:44–53; Acts 1:3–11)

I appeared to my disciples over a period of forty days after my resurrection. My last time with them was in Jerusalem. I said to them, "Everything I told you while I was still with you and everything written about me in the law of Moses, the Prophets and the Psalms had to be fulfilled." I then went on to illuminate the Scripture for their understanding. I pointed out that the Scripture predicted the Christ must suffer and rise from the dead on the third day. I went on to say, "Repentance and forgiveness of sins shall be preached in my name to all the nations. You will begin here in Jerusalem, for you have witnessed all these fulfillments. Don't leave Jerusalem until you receive the promise my Father has made to you. John baptized with water, but you will soon be baptized by the Holy Spirit."

They asked me, "Lord, will you restore the kingdom to Israel at this time?"

I replied, "My Father has decided the times for these things, and they are not for you to know."

I then led them all out to the Mount of Olives as far as Bethany. I said to them, "You will receive power after the Holy Spirit comes upon you so that you will be empowered to be witnesses concerning me to people in Jerusalem, Judea, Samaria and around the world." I then pronounced a blessing on them.

As I finished, I began to rise from the ground. They all gazed up at me until I disappeared into a cloud.

Two men appeared, standing there dressed in white clothing. They said, "Men of Galilee, why do you stand still gazing into the sky? This same Jesus will come back in a similar manner as you have seen him go."

What's your take on it?

Is this your first time reading Jesus' story? Can you find it in yourself to accept that he is who he said he was?

Perhaps you're saying, "What he claimed is outrageous." You're right, it is. If he isn't God like he plainly states, it's more than outrageous—it's blasphemy. The Jewish leaders were right in putting him to death. Who needs a madman running around claiming to be God and convincing people to follow him?

Maybe you don't buy the religious angle. You're thinking, "He couldn't have made these statements—later followers imagined this stuff. They added all the miracles, angels, etc." Maybe you should try writing the story minus the messianic claims, miracles, angels and all. You won't have much left. Certainly, there won't be enough to inspire anyone to bother following him.

If you have never considered the claims Jesus makes, I hope this story bothers you. When you meet the real Jesus, it is very hard to simply dismiss him. If you're bent on doing your own thing, Jesus is very inconvenient, even intimidating. You will probably adopt one of the many excuses for writing him off.

You're taking a big risk.

Suppose he is who he said he was, that the whole story is authentic. Then you had better think again. Jesus says your entire future depends on what you decide about him. "I am the way, the truth and the life. No one can come to the Father (God) except through me." (John 14:6, page 147). Either Jesus is Lord or he is nothing. He doesn't leave you with any other option. If Jesus is Lord, there is no one else worth following compared to him.

I hope you experienced something of the heart of Jesus in this story. "Come to me, everyone who is weary and struggling under heavy burdens, and I will give you rest. (Matthew 11:28, page 102). Jesus is alive, so that is not an empty promise. No matter what you have done, if you make a step toward him, he will come running to embrace you. All you need to do is say from your heart, "Jesus is Lord." You will be forever changed.

We are not naturally anything like Jesus. So you need to let his words soak into your mind, heart and soul. Jesus can liberate you—from legalism, worry, anxiety, fear, anger, hate and even the spirit of control.

One last word: don't judge Jesus by what you have seen of the modern church. Most of us are still too full of ourselves to truly reflect Christ. So look around. When you find the real thing—join them.

Scripture Index

Topical Index

Caesarea Philippi, 73
Caiaphas, 115, 143, 157
Cana, Galilee, 18, 25, 173
Capernaum, 19, 25, 27–32, 46,
    50, 57, 65, 68–70, 77, 92
Centurion's servant, 6
Centurion at the cross, 66
Ceremonial washing, 68, 134
Childlikeness, 102, 118
Children, becoming like, 78,
    118
Children in the marketplace, 48
Children of devil, 87
Children of God, 1, 87, 115, 131
Children praise, 127
Children, tempting them, 78
Chorazin, 92
Christ the Lord, 7
Circumcision, 3, 8, 82
Cleansing the temple, 19–20,
    127
Cleopas, 170
Clopas, 165
Clothes divided, 165
"Come to me", 102
Commandment, greatest, 93,
    132
Commandment, the new, 146–
    147, 150
Condemnation, 21, 96–97, 133,
    134
Cornerstone, chief, 129
Cost, counting the, 106
Covenant, 4,
Crippled woman healed, 100
Cross, taking it up, 62, 74,106
Crown of thorns, 162
Crucifixion, 164–166
"Crucify him", 162–163
Cup of suffering, 121, 155
Cup of water, reward, 62, 78

Dalmanutha, 72
Daniel, 138
David, King, 4, 6, 7, 35, 50, 59,
    83, 122, 127, 132
Day of Preparation, 166
Dead raised, 47, 58, 59, 114, 124
Decapolis, 57, 70
Dedication, feast of, 103
Denial of Jesus, 98
Devil, children of, 87
Disciple, not greater than
    master, 61, 145, 150
Disciples all brethren, 133
Disciples blest, 53, 102, 119,
Disciples chosen by Jesus, 37,
    150
Disciples, gift from the Father,
    154
Disciples lack of faith, 77
Disciples listed, 37–38
Disciples not of this world, 154
Disciples persecuted, 60–61,
    138, 150, 151
Disciples sent out, 60–62, 63
Disciples sent out, the seventy,
    91–92, 102
Disciples, whose greatest, 78,
    144
Discipleship, cost of, 61, 74,
    106, 150–151
Dishonesty, 109
Division in families, 61–62, 100,
    138
Divorce & Remarriage, 40, 110–
    111, 117
Donkey, 93, 102, 105, 125
Doubting Thomas, 166
Dove, 9, 15, 17, 61
Dumb man speaks, 59, 70, 95
Earthquake, 139, 166, 168
Egypt, 11–12

LaVergne, TN USA
30 August 2009
156358LV00004B/2/P